# PAINLESS
# Grammar

**Rebecca Elliott, Ph.D.**

**illustrated by Laurie Hamilton**

BARRON'S

*All inquiries should be addressed to:*
Barron's Educational Series, Inc.
250 Wireless Boulevard
Hauppauge, New York 11788

ISBN-13: 978-0-8120-9781-8
ISBN-10: 0-8120-9781-5

Library of Congress Catalog Card No. 97-7370

**Library of Congress Cataloging-in-Publication Data**

Elliott, Rebecca, 1948–
    Painless grammar / by Rebecca Elliott ; illustrated by Laurie
Hamilton.
        p.   cm.
    Includes index.
    ISBN 0-8120-9781-5
    1. English language—Grammar—Study and teaching.    I. Title.
LB1576.E45 1997
    428'.007—dc21                                                        97-7370
                                                                              CIP


PRINTED IN CANADA
30 29 28 27 26 25 24

*This book is for Josh*

and

Kate and Meg

and

Bill, Emily, Syman, Katie, Marshall, Hartley, Becca,
Tori, Wesley, David, Ryan, Parker,
Robin, Austin, Kacey, Tucker, and Miranda

and

all other kids who want to learn to write right without
being bored to death in the process.

# Acknowledgments

Rule number one of good writing is this: nobody's perfect. Every writer needs editors to give him or her suggestions, make improvements, and point out goofs. Don't be too scared (or too proud) to let other people edit your work—they'll help make you a better writer. Thanks to these editors and advisors of mine: Peter Calingaert, Jim Clark, Jane Danielewicz, Donna Gulick, Emily Sutton, Martha Sutton, Bill Stevens, Joshua Zinn, and Victor Zinn. Special thanks to Richard Lederer, Seth Mirsky, Amy Van Allen and all the other great folks at Barron's, and my husband Jim.

# CONTENTS

# INTRODUCTION

Oh, goody—another grammar book! Who needs another grammar book? Kids, that's who. A user-friendly, action-packed, fun-filled book for kids who want to learn to write well without atrophying their brains from boredom.

When my son was in eighth grade, I volunteered to help his language arts teacher by editing students' papers for their writing lab. It was a joy to go inside the kids' minds to share their thoughts and experiences, but I was distressed that many of them would not have realized, that this sentence contains a totally unnecessary comma. That's one reason I wrote this book.

As I edited the students' papers, I began to wonder, is it possible to teach kids to love to write—and to love to write correctly—without boring them to death? I believe it is, and that's the other reason I wrote *Painless Grammar*. Kids, this book is for you.

Chapter One is entitled "Parts of Speech," but I thought about calling it either "Writing Wrongs" or "Goofs Galore." As you become more familiar with the parts of speech, you'll also become more skilled at using them correctly and avoiding the many errors that sneak into students' writing.

Chapter Two shows you how to weave all those parts of speech into sentences and how to tell a complete sentence from an incomplete sentence. Once you've written a great sentence, you'll learn in this chapter how to punctuate it correctly. Try not to think of punctuation as a bunch of boring rules; think of it as a set of road signs—ways to help your reader navigate easily and comfortably through your writing. If you put punctuation marks, in weird places [as I'm-doing-here]: your reader, soon feels; lost not to "mention" confused and (exasperated).

Chapter Three is on agreement—verbs agreeing with their subjects and pronouns agreeing with their antecedents. After you see all the mistakes students make in this territory, I think you'll agree that agreement is a good thing!

Chapter Four is entitled "Words, Words, Words," and it is a fun ride through some of the wackiest words in the English language and the ways we love to misuse them.

Chapter Five is about editing, which is a fancy word for cleaning up. Messy writing is like a messy room—unattractive and unpleasant. If you know what to look for, cleaning up your writing is easy and fun.

Kids, I hope this book will help you write better and get higher grades in language arts class, but much more importantly, I hope it will help unleash your creativity, set your imagination on fire, and show you the pleasure that can come from expressing your ideas with clarity and style.

# CHAPTER ONE

# Parts of Speech

# NOUN POINTERS

## What is a noun?

It is a word that names a person, place, thing, idea, or quality.

| | |
|---|---|
| **Person** | boy, teacher, Josh, doctor |
| **Place** | Miami, city, countryside |
| **Thing** | house, tree, horse, bicycle, ice cream |
| **Idea** | democracy, truth, illusion, fantasy |
| **Quality** | beauty, caring, hatred, boredom |

We use <u>nouns</u> all the <u>time</u> when we write <u>letters</u> to <u>friends</u> or <u>papers</u> for <u>class</u>. (For <u>example</u>, all these underlined <u>words</u> are <u>nouns</u>.) In the next few <u>pages</u>, we'll look at some <u>mistakes</u> that <u>students</u> frequently make with <u>nouns</u>—and I'll give you <u>pointers</u> on how to avoid making those <u>mistakes</u> when you write.

## When to capitalize nouns

### Names of specific people

<u>CAPS:</u>
   Tucker, Tori, Juanita, Denzel, the Stevens family, the Joneses
<u>NO CAPS:</u>
   family, boy, girl, sister, cousin

What about mom and dad? Capitalize them when you're calling your parent's name but not when you refer to "my mom" or "my dad."

<u>CAPS:</u>
   Hi, Mom! Welcome home, Dad.
<u>NO CAPS:</u>
   My father and my mother are busy. Could your mom or your dad drive us to the movie?

## Days of the week, months, and holidays, but not seasons

CAPS:
Monday, December, Passover, Easter
NO CAPS:
autumn, fall, spring, winter, summer

## Ranks and titles, but only when used with a particular person's name

CAPS:
This is Doctor Smith, this is Aunt Anne, and that man is General Bradshaw.
NO CAPS:
That man is my doctor, that woman is my aunt, and that man is a general in the army.

## Geographic areas: cities, states, countries, counties, rivers, oceans, streets, parks, etc.

CAPS:
North Dakota, Ohio River, Atlantic Ocean, Franklin Street, Umstead Park, Lake Jordan, Rocky Mountains
NO CAPS:
The ocean is deep. The mountains are high.

## Regions of the United States, but not simple directions

CAPS:
I was born in the Midwest, but I grew up in the North.
NO CAPS:
I live on the north side of town.

## Historical periods

CAPS:
the Renaissance, World War II, the Middle Ages, the Civil War
NO CAPS:
It was a long war. We live in an age of computers.

## Religions, nationalities, races of people, languages, countries and adjectives related to those countries

CAPS:
Christians, Jews, Asians, Africans, Japanese, Arabic, France, French fries, Germany, German measles

## The various names for God and the names of sacred books

CAPS:
God, Jehovah, Allah, the Bible, the Koran
NO CAPS:
There were many gods and goddesses in ancient myths.

## Specific school courses, but not general subjects

CAPS:
I'm taking Algebra 101 and History of China.
NO CAPS:
I'm taking algebra and history.

## Names of specific schools, businesses, buildings, organizations, etc.

### CAPS:
Apple Computer, Phillips Middle School, the University of Ohio

### NO CAPS:
I want a new computer. That building is a middle school. I plan to attend a university.

## Brand names

### CAPS:
Chevrolet Camaro, Nintendo, Cheerios, Nestle's Crunch

## Names of planets, but not sun and moon and sometimes not earth

### CAPS:
Jupiter, Mars, Neptune, Earth (capitalized when you're referring to it as one of the planets)

### NO CAPS:
The moon is full tonight. More than five billion people live on the earth.

## Letters that stand alone

### CAPS:
U-turn, T-shirt, X-ray, an A$^+$ in social studies class

## Names of specific teams and clubs and their members

### CAPS:
the Atlanta Braves, the Republican Party, Republicans

### NO CAPS:
I play on a baseball team.

## Titles of movies, books, chapters, and articles

### CAPS:
*Jurassic Park*, "Tar Heels Beat Duke 102-96," *Gulliver's Travels*

NO CAPS:

>Little words (articles, conjunctions, and short prepositions) are usually not capitalized unless
>
>- they are the beginning word: *The Life and Times of King Joshua the Great*
>- they are part of the verb: "Thief Holds Up Bank" (*Up* is not a preposition; it is part of the verb *to hold up*.)

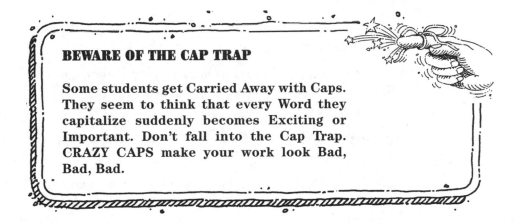

**BEWARE OF THE CAP TRAP**

Some students get Carried Away with Caps. They seem to think that every Word they capitalize suddenly becomes Exciting or Important. Don't fall into the Cap Trap. CRAZY CAPS make your work look Bad, Bad, Bad.

# Making nouns possessive

When we want to show that someone owns something, we use possessive nouns.

>The nose of Mary = Mary's nose
>The toes of Gary = Gary's toes

To make a noun possessive, usually add an apostrophe and an *s*.

| Noun | Possessive |
| --- | --- |
| Juanita | Juanita's cat |
| cat | the cat's tail |
| Boris | Boris's mustache |

Most of the exceptions to this rule are old-fashioned or historical names:

RIGHT:
Jesus' parables
RIGHT:
Moses' tablets
RIGHT:
Achilles' heel

If two people own the same thing, use an apostrophe and *s* for only the second person.

Adam and Debbie's marriage (they share one marriage)
Clinton and Gore's administration (they share one administration)

If the two people don't own the same thing, use an apostrophe and *s* for both people.

Adam's and Debbie's toes (they don't share the same toes)
Clinton's and Gore's careers (they don't share the same careers)

## Showing possession when the noun is plural

If the plural ends in *s* (for example, *boys*) just add an apostrophe. If the plural does not end in *s* (for example, *women*) add an apostrophe and an *s*.

| One person, one item | Two people, two items |
| --- | --- |
| the boy's jacket | the boys' jackets |
| my parent's car | my parents' cars |
| my boss's hat | my bosses' hats |
| the woman's dress | the women's dresses |
| the child's toy | the children's toys |
| the passerby's glance | the passersby's glances |

Inanimate objects usually don't own things, but some possessives are okay.

| | |
|---|---|
| one month's vacation | two months' vacation |
| one dollar's worth | two dollars' worth |
| the razor's edge | the two razors' edges |
| the chair's leg | the chairs' legs |

What about the example *the chair's leg*? It's okay, but in formal writing it should be *the chair leg* or *the leg of the chair*. The same is true with this example:

<u>OKAY:</u>
   my bike's tire
<u>BETTER:</u>
   my bike tire (I own the tire—the bike doesn't own it.)
<u>ALSO GOOD:</u>
   the tire on my bike

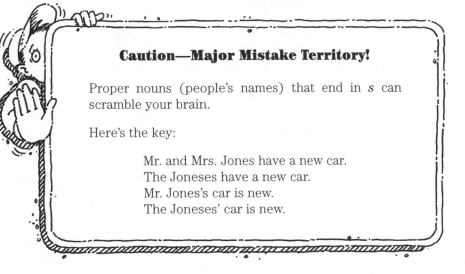

### Caution—Major Mistake Territory!

Proper nouns (people's names) that end in *s* can scramble your brain.

Here's the key:

> Mr. and Mrs. Jones have a new car.
> The Joneses have a new car.
> Mr. Jones's car is new.
> The Joneses' car is new.

> ✔ **Check this out:**
>
> The kid's bike = one kid, one bike
> The kids' bike = two (or more) kids
>    sharing the same bike
> The kids' bikes = two (or more) kids with
>    different bikes

## Making nouns plural

One book, two <u>books</u>; one hat, two <u>hats</u>—what's the big deal?
We make <u>words</u> plural all the time. So you think <u>plurals</u> are
a piece of cake? Most are, but look at some of these
<u>troublemakers</u>:

| | | | | |
|---|---|---|---|---|
| If it's | house—houses | | If it's | box—boxes |
| Why is it | mouse—mice | | Why is it | ox—oxen |
| | | | | |
| If it's | hero—heroes | | If it's | safe—safes |
| Why it is | banjo—banjos | | Why is it | knife—knives |
| | | | | |
| If it's | cupful—cupfuls | | Go figure: | foot—feet |
| Why is it | passerby—passersby | | | child—children |
| | | | | tooth—teeth |
| | | | | man—men |
| | | | | woman—women |

There are no absolute rules for plurals. If you are uncertain,
check your dictionary. It will tell you the correct plural for
each word.

A few nouns stay the same no matter whether you're talking about one of them or a thousand of them. Check these out:

| Singular | Plural | Singular | Plural |
|----------|--------|----------|--------|
| moose | moose | sheep | sheep |
| deer | deer | series | series |
| species | species | swine | swine |

The plurals of some words are based on rules from foreign languages; you either have to memorize them or look them up.

| Singular | Plural | Singular | Plural |
|----------|--------|----------|--------|
| basis | bases | nucleus | nuclei |
| crisis | crises | stimulus | stimuli |
| criterion | criteria | datum | data |

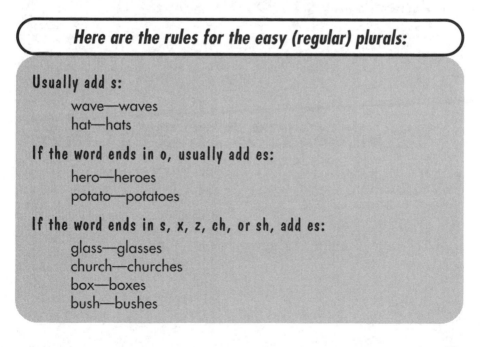

## Here are the rules for the easy (regular) plurals:

**Usually add s:**
   wave—waves
   hat—hats

**If the word ends in o, usually add es:**
   hero—heroes
   potato—potatoes

**If the word ends in s, x, z, ch, or sh, add es:**
   glass—glasses
   church—churches
   box—boxes
   bush—bushes

## Rules for the easy (regular) plurals (continued)

If the word ends in y and there's a vowel (a, e, i, o, or u) before the y, add s:

> play—plays
> monkey—monkeys

If the word ends in y and there's a consonant before the y, change the y to i and add es:

> party—parties
> duty—duties

If a proper noun (someone's name) ends in y, just add s:

> the Kennedy family—the Kennedys
> the Finley family—the Finleys

If a compound noun (a noun containing more than one word) has a main noun in it, add the s to the main noun:

> one father-in-law, two fathers-in-law
> one chief of staff, two chiefs of staff

If a compound noun has no main noun in it, add the s at the end:

> one follow-up, two follow-ups
> one trade-in, two trade-ins

## Just for fun

If this is right — one goose, two geese
Then why shouldn't we say — one moose, two meese

If this is right — one die, two dice
Then why shouldn't we say — one pie, two pice
And — one lie, two lice

If this is right — one sheep, two sheep
Then why shouldn't we say — one creep, two creep

| | |
|---|---|
| **If this is right** | one cherub, two cherubim |
| Then why shouldn't we say | one bathtub, two bathtubim |
| | |
| **If this is right** | one foot, two feet |
| Then why shouldn't we say | one root, two reet |
| And | one boot, two beet |
| | |
| **If this is right** | one man, two men |
| Then why shouldn't we say | one pan, two pen |
| And | one fan, two fen |
| And | one can, two cen |
| | |
| **If this is right** | one tooth, two teeth |
| Then why shouldn't we say | one telephone booth, two |
| | telephone beeth |

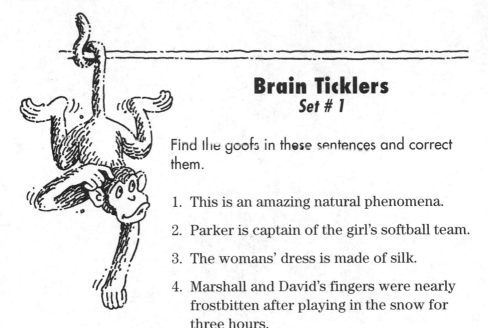

## Brain Ticklers
### Set # 1

Find the goofs in these sentences and correct them.

1. This is an amazing natural phenomena.

2. Parker is captain of the girl's softball team.

3. The womans' dress is made of silk.

4. Marshall and David's fingers were nearly frostbitten after playing in the snow for three hours.

5. I asked dad to drive me to Emily's house.

6. I really Really want to go to the Brand New Mall and see whether they sell Neat Stuff!

7. I heard the babie's cries.

8. I borrowed my bosses car for an hour because mine was in the shop.

9. I grew up in the south.

10. The City where Batman lives is Gotham City.

(Answers are on page 59.)

# PRONOUN POINTERS

## What is a pronoun?

It is a word that stands in for a noun.

Pronouns are handy little critters. If you don't believe me, just try talking without them.

GIMME A BREAK:

Parker gave Parker's dog the dog's bath.

MUCH SIMPLER:

Parker gave <u>her</u> dog <u>its</u> bath.

GIMME A BREAK:

Please say the name of the person on the other end of this telephone.

MUCH SIMPLER:

<u>Who</u> are <u>you</u>? <u>What</u> is <u>your</u> name?

GIMME A BREAK:

The person named Katie sitting in that chair likes the person named Sue sitting in that chair.

MUCH SIMPLER:

<u>She</u> likes <u>her</u>.

## Here are the ways we use pronouns:

- to name specific people or things: <u>You</u> look like <u>him</u>.
- to point to non-specific people or things: <u>Everyone</u> enjoyed the party, but <u>nobody</u> remembered to thank the hostess.
- to point to something: <u>This</u> is the dress I want.
- to refer back to the subject: Bruce hurt <u>himself</u>.
- to show mutual action: Ryan and Wesley were wrestling and hurt <u>each</u> <u>other</u>.
- to add emphasis: I <u>myself</u> love intensive pronouns.

15

- to ask a question: <u>Who</u> is that?
- to show ownership: That's not <u>yours</u>; it's <u>mine</u>!

## Watching out for crazy antecedents

A pronoun takes the place of a noun. The antecedent is the noun that the pronoun takes the place of or stands for.

> I am Kristen.
> > *I* is a pronoun. Who or what does it stand for? It stands for *Kristen.* The antecedent of *I* is *Kristen.*

> Tucker gave his sister her doll.
> > *His* is a pronoun. Who does it stand for? It stands for *Tucker,* so the antecedent of *his* is *Tucker.* The word *her* is also a pronoun and it stands for *sister.* The antecedent of *her* is *sister.*

The pronoun almost always refers to the noun closest to it. If you put pronouns in odd places, it's hard to tell what the antecedent is. Sometimes sentences can get pretty crazy.

**CRAZY:**
> It was pitch dark and my cat was still outdoors. I grabbed my flashlight to begin the search and listened for its purr.

(The antecedent of *its* appears to be *flashlight.* What's wrong with this picture: a purring flashlight?)

**BETTER:**

It was pitch dark and my cat was still outdoors. I grabbed my flashlight to begin the search and listened for Magic's purr.

**CRAZY:**

There was a knock at the door. It was my mother.

(*It* seems to refer to the knock, so the sentence seems to say that the knock at the door was my mother. I don't know about your mother, but my mother is a woman, not a knock.)

**BETTER:**

There was a knock at the door. My mother had arrived.

**CRAZY:**

While driving it at 200 mph around the North Pole, Santa swerved to avoid hitting an elf and landed his sleigh in a snowdrift.

(The pronoun *it* appears early in this sentence, but we don't find out what *it* is until the end of the sentence— and by that time we have an elf and a snowdrift to deal with as well.)

**BETTER:**

While driving his sleigh at 200 mph around the North Pole, Santa swerved to avoid hitting an elf and landed in a snowdrift.

**CRAZY:**

I've been to Mexico, and I like them because they are very kind to Americans.

(The antecedent has been left out of this sentence. Who are *they*?)

**BETTER:**

I've been to Mexico, and I like the Mexicans because they are very kind to Americans.

# When is Josh a "him" and when is he a "he"?

Which is correct?

> I like you better than him.
> I like you better than he.

Both are correct, but they mean entirely different things.

> I like you better than him = I like you better than I like him.
> I like you better than he = I like you better than he likes you.

## Pronouns come in three groups called cases.

> *Subjective case*—the doer (subject) of the action:
> I throw the ball.
> *Objective case*—the receiver (object) of the action:
> Throw the ball to me.
> *Possessive case*—shows ownership:
> My throw to third base won the game!

| Subjective Case | Objective Case | Possessive Case |
|---|---|---|
| I sing. | Sing to me. | my song |
| You sing. | Joe sings to you. | your song |
| She sings. | Sing to her. | her song |
| He sings. | Sing to him. | his song |
| It sings. | Sing to it. | its song |
| We sing. | Sing to us. | our song |
| They sing. | Sing to them. | their song |
| Who sings? | To whom does Joe sing? | whose song |

## What is wrong with these sentences?

> Mom cooked dinner for Brian and I.
> Her and I went to the mall after school.
> Us eighth graders are studying algebra.
> She is taller than me.

Each of the underlined pronouns is wrong. How can you tell whether to use a subjective pronoun or an objective pronoun? Add more words to the sentence (or delete words) until you can tell which pronoun sounds right.

**ADD WORDS:**
Mom cooked dinner for Brian and (for) I. Sounds wrong.
Mom cooked dinner for Brian and (for) me. Much better.
**RIGHT:**
Mom cooked dinner for Brian and me.

**ADD WORDS:**
Her (went) and I went to the mall after school. Sounds wrong.
She (went) and I went to the mall after school. Much better.
**RIGHT:**
She and I went to the mall after school.

**DELETE WORDS:**
Us (eighth graders) are studying algebra. Sounds wrong.
We (eighth graders) are studying algebra. Much better.
**RIGHT:**
We eighth graders are studying algebra.

**ADD WORDS:**
She is taller than me (am tall). Sounds wrong.
She is taller than I (am tall). Much better.
**RIGHT:**
She is taller than I.

## Here is another trick to use when you are confused: turn the sentence around and notice what sounds right.

In language arts, the best students are Ryan and (me/I).
**TURN IT AROUND:**
Me am the best student. Sounds wrong.
I am the best student. Much better.
**RIGHT:**
In language arts, the best students are Ryan and I.

19

The winner of the award for fastest pizza eater is (he/him).

**TURN IT AROUND:**
Him is the winner. Sounds wrong.
He is the winner. Much better.

**RIGHT:**
The winner of the award for fastest pizza eater is he.

# Polite pronouns

## It is considered polite to put yourself second.

**WRONG:**
Me and Mike want to go to town.
**RIGHT BUT NOT SO POLITE:**
I and Mike want to go to town.
**POLITE:**
Mike and I want to go to town.

**WRONG:**
Mom gave the cookies to her and I.
**RIGHT BUT NOT SO POLITE:**
Mom gave the cookies to me and her.
**POLITE:**
Mom gave the cookies to her and me.

## Is it *me* or is it *I*? It's a hot debate.

| Is this right? | Or is this right? |
| --- | --- |
| It's me. | It's I. |
| It's him. | It's he. |
| It's her. | It's she. |
| It's us. | It's we. |
| It's them. | It's they. |

Even the experts don't agree on this one. According to the strictest rules, *it's me* is wrong. (Turn the sentences around. You would never say "me am it" or "her is it." You would say "I am it" and "she is it.") However, *it's me* is so commonly used that it is gaining acceptance as an idiom. In informal speech or writing, it's okay, but in formal writing or public speaking, use *it's I*.

## The ubiquitous *you*

*Ubiquitous* means "it's everywhere! it's everywhere!" *You* is one of the most overused words in our language. In formal writing, be careful. When using the word *you*, the writer should really mean "you, the reader," not someone, anyone, or everyone.

INFORMAL:
> If you add one and one, you get two.

FORMAL:
> One plus one equals two.

INFORMAL:
> You have to pay $3.50 to get into the movie.

FORMAL:
> The movie costs $3.50.

INFORMAL:
> If you're late for school, you'll get in trouble.

FORMAL:
> Students who are late for school will get in trouble.

INFORMAL:
> You have to pay taxes when you grow up.

FORMAL:
> All people have to pay taxes when they grow up.

# BRAIN TICKLERS
## Set # 2

Find the goofs in these sentences and correct them.

1. Susan remembered to bring Mary's jacket to school but forgot her gloves.

2. They don't allow kids to throw jello at each other in the cafeteria.

3. When doing a plié, the ballerina should keep her knees over her toes. You shouldn't allow your knees to turn inward or one could damage one's knees and ankles.

4. I gave Todd a new bike and a video game; it made him happy.

5. Hello. You want to speak to Marianne? This is her.

6. We had a great time at Myrtle Beach; they have so much to do there.

7. The teacher told we kids to be quiet.

8. We're going out to dinner alone—just Erica and me.

9. It was him who ate all the nachos.

10. Mom gave both of us, Elizabeth and I, money for the movie.

11. Tucker is a friend of Miranda's and me.

(Answers are on page 60.)

# VERB POINTERS

## What is a verb?

It is a word that shows action or state of being.

- action: run, swim, jump, taste, fall, dream
- state of being: be, appear, seem, feel

I can make plenty of interesting sentences without nouns. For example:

> Don't do that. It's dangerous and if you do it enough, it'll kill you!
> He likes her, but I like him more than she does.
> Listen closely to what I say and you'll learn to write right.

Not bad, huh? I dare you to make a juicy sentence without a verb. Okay, sentence fragments maybe:

> Wow! What a great bike.
> Yumm. Good food. More cookies anywhere?

But how long can you live on fragments? Try writing a real sentence without verbs.

> There no way we without verbs. Nothing. Without any action words, our sentences . . . dead. No communication. Action . . . being . . . without them, well, *nothing.*

We need verbs! Here are some ways to treat verbs with respect and to avoid the verb goofs students often make.

## Verb tenses

### Verb tenses let us know when the action happens.

PRESENT TENSE:
> I *ace* tests sometimes, but not often enough.

PRESENT PROGRESSIVE TENSE:
> I *am acing* this test right this minute!

<u>PAST TENSE:</u>
I *aced* the test yesterday.
<u>FUTURE TENSE:</u>
I know I *will ace* the test tomorrow.

Be consistent with tenses. If you think clearly about what you're trying to say, usually the choice of verb tenses will be obvious.

<u>WEAK:</u>
I got home late and Mom fusses at me for not calling to let her know where I will be.
I got home = past tense
Mom fusses = present tense
where I will be = future tense

<u>BETTER:</u>
I got home late and Mom fussed at me for not calling to let her know where I had been.
I got home = past tense
Mom fussed = past tense
where I had been = past perfect tense

## Here are the six tenses you have to choose from:

Present tense: I *eat* pizza often.
Past tense: I *ate* pizza last night.
Future tense: I *will eat* pizza later today.
Present perfect tense: I *have eaten* pizza many times.
Past perfect tense: I *had eaten* pizza just before you arrived.
Future perfect tense: I *will have eaten* pizza at least a million times by the year 2000.

## Here are the six progressive forms. (Progressive means that the action continues for a while.)

Present progressive: I *am eating* pizza.
Past progressive: I *was eating* pizza when you called.
Future progressive: I *will be eating* pizza at 8:30 tonight.
Present perfect progressive: I *have been eating* pizza all day.
Past perfect progressive: I *had been eating* pizza for three hours when Mom said my eyeballs looked like pepperonis.

Future perfect progressive: I *will have been eating* pizza for five hours nonstop when bedtime rolls around.

## Here are the three uses of the emphatic form:

Emphasis: I *do eat* pizza! When I was a kid, wow, *did* I *eat* pizza.

Questions: *Do* I *eat* pizza? *Did* I really *eat* 25 pizzas?

Negatives: I *do not eat* green, leafy vegetables—only pizza. However, I *did not eat* all 25 pizzas by myself.

## When to use the present tense:

Present action: I *want* to eat pizza right now.

Action that happens over and over: I *eat* pizza almost every day.

Scientific facts and other things that are always true: Eating 25 pizzas a day *is* not good for you.

Headlines: "Local Kid Nearly *Explodes* from Pizza Overdose"

Sometimes the present tense is used in place of the future tense: Tomorrow I *leave* for a special hospital to try to overcome my pizza addiction.

In book reports (stories often occur "in the present" as a reader reads them): In the final scenes of *Pizza Panic*, the hero of the story *is* cured of his pizza addiction and *lives* happily ever after, never again craving mozzarella and pepperoni.

# Split infinitives

An infinitive is a verb with the word *to* in front of it. Splitting an infinitive means putting one or more words between *to* and the verb.

| Infinitive | Non-split infinitive | Split infinitive |
|---|---|---|
| to run | to run quickly | to quickly run |
| to swim | to swim eagerly | to eagerly swim |
| to jump | to jump determinedly | to determinedly jump |

WEAK:
> It is usually better <u>to</u> not <u>split</u> infinitives.

BETTER:
> It is usually better not <u>to</u> <u>split</u> infinitives.

Split the infinitive when you want to emphasize the word or words in between.

RIGHT:
> I want you <u>to</u> <u>study</u> the material for the test.

MORE EMPHASIS:
> I want you <u>to</u> thoroughly <u>study</u> the material for the test.

When you split an infinitive, be careful not to put too many words between *to* and the verb.

CONFUSING:
> I want you <u>to</u> thoroughly and deliberately, without cutting any corners or making any excuses, <u>study</u> for the test.

BETTER:
> I want you <u>to</u> thoroughly and deliberately <u>study</u> for the test without cutting any corners or making any excuses.

# Is your voice active or passive?

Most writers and editors dislike the passive voice. They say it's too blah.

**PASSIVE VOICE:**
> The ball was hit.
> (By whom? The passive voice hides the doer of the action.)

**ACTIVE VOICE:**
> Tucker hit the ball.

**PASSIVE VOICE:**
> Cigarette taxes will be raised.
> (By whom?)

**ACTIVE VOICE:**
> Congress will raise taxes on cigarettes.

**PASSIVE VOICE:**
> My nose was punched by you.
> (At least we know who did it, but nobody talks this way.)

**ACTIVE VOICE:**
> You punched me in the nose!

You can see from these examples that the passive voice is less dynamic than the active voice because it ignores or downplays the doer of the action. Imagine you are a sportswriter. Which voice do you think your readers would find most interesting?

**PASSIVE VOICE:**
> The ball was hit and a run was scored. The score was kept and eventually the game was won. Strong emotions were felt by the fans and much applause was heard.

**ACTIVE VOICE:**
> In the bottom of the ninth inning, Slugger Batson slammed the ball across the fence, and every player on the previously loaded bases slid home. Our team won 10-8! The crowd went wild!

## The passive voice is often better in these cases:

• The doer of the action is not important or not known.

**PASSIVE VOICE:**
> School is canceled today!
> (Who cares who canceled it?)

**PASSIVE VOICE:**
The cafeteria food was contaminated.
(Nobody knows who contaminated it.)

• You want to be polite, avoid sounding bossy, or soften a strong statement.

**PASSIVE VOICE:**
Your application was rejected.
**ACTIVE VOICE:**
We rejected your application.

**PASSIVE VOICE:**
The test must be finished in one hour.
**ACTIVE VOICE:**
You must finish the test in one hour.

• You want to emphasize the thing you're talking about, not the person who does the action.

**PASSIVE VOICE:**
This big blue ribbon [emphasizing the thing] will be given to the winner.
**ACTIVE VOICE:**
The winner [emphasizing the person] will receive this big blue ribbon.

• You are writing in an impersonal, scientific manner.

**PASSIVE VOICE:**
The mice were separated into two groups.
**ACTIVE VOICE:**
My lab partner and I separated the mice into two groups.

# Gerunds

**If you put *-ing* on the end of a verb, you can turn the verb into a noun—and that noun is called a gerund.**

I run [verb]. Running [noun/gerund] is fun.
I eat [verb] ice cream. Eating [noun/gerund] ice cream is even more fun than running [noun/gerund].

## Possessive nouns and pronouns (ones that show ownership) are usually used with gerunds.

WRONG:

Mom doesn't like me eating too much ice cream.

RIGHT:

Mom doesn't like my eating too much ice cream.

WRONG:

Josh smacking his chewing gum is driving me crazy.

RIGHT:

Josh's smacking his chewing gum is driving me crazy.

## If the emphasis is on the action, always use the possessive case.

(See page 18 for more on the possessive case.)

I hope you don't mind my eating the apple.

## But if you want to strongly emphasize the doer of the action, you have the option of using the objective case.

(See page 18 for more on the objective case.)

I hope you don't mind me holding your hand. (I'm glad it's just *me* holding your hand—not the other girls!)

# The subjunctive mood

<u>WRONG:</u>
> I were born in 1979.

<u>RIGHT:</u>
> I was born in 1979.

This is obvious, right? Sure it is—at least most of the time. Sometimes we do say "if I were" or "if she were." This is called the subjunctive mood.

## Here is a trick for telling whether to use the subjunctive mood: If the sentence is a *what if* or *if only* sentence, use the subjunctive.

<u>WHAT IF:</u>
> If <u>I</u> <u>were</u> a magician, I would turn the entire world into chocolate.

<u>WHAT IF:</u>
> If <u>she</u> <u>were</u> to win the $10 million lottery, what do you think she would do with the money?

<u>IF ONLY:</u>
> If <u>I</u> <u>were</u> an eagle, I would soar high above mountains and deep into canyons. I've wished many times that <u>I</u> <u>were</u> an eagle.

<u>IF ONLY:</u>
> If <u>he</u> <u>were</u> 16, my boyfriend would be able to drive.

<u>BACK TO REALITY:</u>
> I think <u>I</u> <u>was</u> 17 when my grandmother died. But if <u>I</u> <u>was</u> 16 when it happened, then the year would have been 1987. (This is a statement of fact, not *what if.*)

<u>MORE REALITY:</u>
> If <u>it</u> <u>was</u> snowing yesterday in the Northeast as much as the weather forecaster had predicted, I bet the kids there don't have school today. (This is a statement of fact, not *what if.*)

## The subjunctive is also used for suggestions, commands, urgency, and recommendations.

STATEMENT:

School <u>is</u> canceled.

SUGGESTION:

I politely suggest that school <u>be</u> canceled forever.

STATEMENT:

Darnell <u>eats</u> all ten bagels.

COMMAND:

I command that Darnell <u>eat</u> all ten bagels that he ordered.

STATEMENT :

Juan <u>gives</u> his homework attention.

URGENCY:

It is essential that Juan <u>give</u> his homework more attention.

STATEMENT :

We <u>are</u> finished with subjunctives.

RECOMMENDATION:

I vote that we <u>be</u> finished with subjunctives.

## Some tricky irregular verbs

> **Here is the format for the following examples:**
>
> Today I ___.    Yesterday I ___.    Many times I have___.

## Regular verbs work this way:

| Today | Yesterday | Many times |
|---|---|---|
| cook | cooked | cooked |
| fix | fixed | fixed |
| pick | picked | picked |
| jump | jumped | jumped |

Regular verbs are a piece of cake. Unfortunately, irregular verbs aren't so easy.

Sometimes there's a pattern to irregular verbs.

| Today | Yesterday | Many times |
|---|---|---|
| blow | blew | blown |
| grow | grew | grown |
| know | knew | known |
| throw | threw | thrown |
| sell | sold | sold |
| tell | told | told |

Sometimes there's no pattern.

| Today | Yesterday | Many times |
|---|---|---|
| ride | rode | ridden |
| slide | slid | slid |
| wake | woke | woken |
| take | took | taken |
| make | made | made |
| eat | ate | eaten |
| beat | beat | beaten |

Sometimes you think there's a pattern, then along comes a surprise.

|  | Today | Yesterday | Many times |
|---|---|---|---|
| If it's | drink | drank | drunk |
| and it's | sink | sank | sunk |
| and it's | shrink | shrank | shrunk |
| why is it | think | thought | thought |
| If it's | sing | sang | sung |
| and it's | ring | rang | rung |
| and it's | spring | sprang | sprung |
| why is it | fling | flung | flung |

## Troubling Verbs

If you grew up speaking English, you know that we say "the teacher taught," but we don't say "the preacher praught." Your ear will tell you that it's fine to say that you "wrote your sister," but it's not fine to say that you "bote your sister" if what you did was bite her. You know most irregular verbs by ear, but here are a few troublemakers. (When two words are given, either is okay but the first choice is a little better.)

Bite, bit, bitten or bit
Bring, brought, brought—*brang* and *brung* are not words
Drag, dragged, dragged—*drug* is often used but not correct
Dive, dived or dove, dived
Drive, drove, driven—*drived* is not a word
Forget, forgot, forgotten or forgot
Get, got, gotten or got
Hang (to hang a picture or to dangle): hang, hung, hung
Hang (to hang a horse thief): hang, hanged, hanged
Hide, hid, hid or hidden

## Troubling Verbs (continued)

Kneel, knelt or kneeled, knelt or kneeled
Leap, leaped or leapt, leaped or leapt
Light, lighted or lit, lighted or lit
Prove, proved, proved or proven
Rise, rose, risen—*rised* is not a word
Shine (to polish, as in to shine silver): shine, shined, shined
Shine (to give off light like a star): shine, shone, shone
Shrink, shrank or shrunk, shrunk or shrunken
Sing, sang or sung, sung
Sink, sank or sunk, sunk—*sinked* is not a word
Spring, sprang or sprung, sprung
Stink, stank or stunk, stunk
Sweat, sweat or sweated, sweat or sweated
Swim, swam, swum
Swing, swung, swung
Tread, trod or treaded, trodden or trod
Wake, woke or waked, waked or woken

### Caution—Major Mistake Territory!

Many adults get confused about the difference between *lie* and *lay*, too.

## Lie and lay

People lie on beds. Dogs lie on people. Fleas lie on dogs. The people, the dogs, and the fleas are very still. *Lie* is a still verb.

A person picks up a dog and lays it on a blanket. A pair of tweezers picks a flea off a dog and lays it outside. A hen lays an

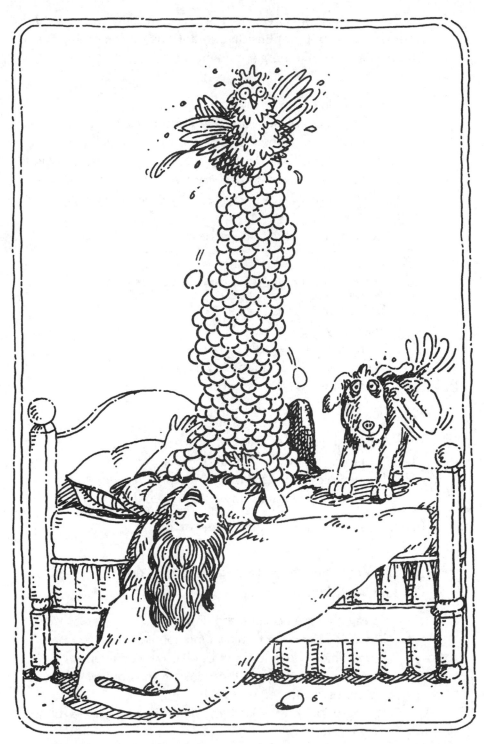

egg. The person, the tweezers, and the hen are very active. *Lay* is an active verb. It implies that somebody or something is setting or placing something somewhere.

**WRONG:**

I will lie the baby in the crib.

(When in doubt, substitute the word *place* or *put*. If the sentence sounds right, the verb you want is *lay*. If it doesn't sound right, *lie* is the right verb. I will place the baby in the crib. In other words, I will *lay* the baby in the crib. After I *lay* the baby in the crib, the baby itself will *lie* in the crib.)

RIGHT:

I will lay the baby in the crib.

## Lie (to lie down on a bed): lie, lay, lain, lying

Today I lie in bed.
Yesterday I lay in bed.
Many times I have lain in bed.
Yesterday I was lying in bed all day.
Lying in bed all day is boring.

Pick the correct verb:

I'm tired; I need to (lay/lie) down.
I (laid/lay) down for about an hour.
I have (laid/lain) here long enough; I'm ready to get up.
I am (laying/lying) on my sister's bed.

In each case, the second choice is correct.

## Lay (to place something, to set something down): lay, laid, laid, laying

Today I lay the book on the counter.
Yesterday I laid the book on the counter.
Many times I have laid the book on the counter.
Yesterday I was laying the book on the counter when Mom came home.
Laying books on the kitchen counter is against the rules in my house.

Pick the correct verb:

> Katie, please (lie/lay) the book on the table.
> Katie obeyed and (lay/laid) the book on the table.
> She has (lain/laid) it where I asked.
> Now Katie is (lying/laying) another book on the table.

In each case, the second choice is correct.

## Lie (to tell a fib): lie, lied, lied, lying

### RIGHT:

> I think he's lying. He told the police he had been lying in
> bed all night near his buddy, who lay on the couch.
> Meanwhile, the smoking pistol lay in the straw near the
> hens laying eggs in the coop. I'm sure he's lied many
> times about where he's lain after laying the pistol, still hot
> from the crime, in some sneaky place. What a lying liar!

## Just for fun

| If this is right | today he speaks, yesterday he spoke |
| Then why don't we say | the faucet leaks, yesterday it loke |

| If this is right | today I do, yesterday I did |
| Then why don't we say | today cows moo, yesterday they mid |
| And | today I boo-hoo, yesterday I bid-hid |

| If this is right | today I see, yesterday I saw |
| Then why don't we say | today I flee, yesterday I flaw |
| And | today I agree, yesterday I agraw |
| And | today I guarantee, yesterday I guarantaw |

| If this is right | today you win, yesterday you won |
| Then why don't we say | today you sin, yesterday you son |
| And | the seamstresses pin, yesterday they pon |

| If this is right | you strike the ball, yesterday you struck it |

|                        |                                                  |
|------------------------|--------------------------------------------------|
| Then why don't we say  | you hike the ball, yesterday you huck it         |
| And                    | you like the pie, yesterday you luck it          |
|                        |                                                  |
| **If this is right**   | today I take, yesterday I took                   |
| Then why don't we say  | today I make, yesterday I mook                   |
| And                    | today I bake, yesterday I book                   |
|                        |                                                  |
| **If this is right**   | today I think, yesterday I thought               |
| Then why don't we say  | today I sink, yesterday I sought                 |
|                        |                                                  |
| **If this is right**   | he eats the cake, yesterday he ate it            |
| Then why don't we say  | he beats the egg, yesterday he bate it           |
| And                    | the vet treats the dog, yesterday he trate it    |
|                        |                                                  |
| **If this is right**   | today you fly, yesterday you flew                |
| Then why don't we say  | today you cry, yesterday you crew                |
|                        |                                                  |
| **If this is right**   | today I freeze, yesterday I froze                |
| Then why don't we say  | today I sneeze, yesterday I snoze                |
|                        |                                                  |
| **If this is right**   | today I sit, yesterday I sat                     |
| Then why don't we say  | the dress doesn't fit, but yesterday it fat      |

●●●●●●●●●●●●●●●●●●●●●●●●●●●●●●●●●●●●●●●●●●●●●●●●

## BRAIN TICKLERS
### Set # 3

Find the goofs in these sentences and correct them.

1. Mom fusses a lot about me trashing my room.

2. When I was a kid, I swang every day on an old tire my dad hanged in a tree for me.

3. I wish I'd waken up earlier.

4. Adam breaks the dish when he tossed it to Omar who is standing at the sink.

5. If I was you, I'd buy that gorgeous dress.

6. I've laid awake all night worrying about my math test.

7. I worked for three hours, and finally the assignment was completed.

8. My mom screamed, "I can't stand you splitting infinitives!"

9. If you want to really, truly, without a doubt thrill your teacher, don't split infinitives.

10. The headline read, "Local Kid Won Scholarship from Pizza Hut."

(Answers are on page 62.)

# ADJECTIVE AND ADVERB POINTERS

## What is an adjective?

It is a word that describes a noun or a pronoun and tells these things:

- which one: this, that
- what kind: red, large, sick, cloudy, enormous, petite
- how many: six, four hundred, many, several

## What is an adverb?

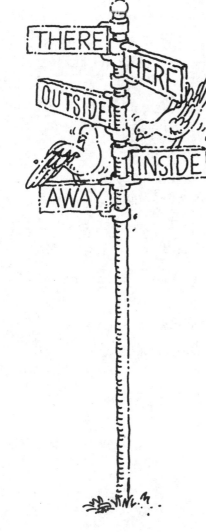

It is a word that describes a verb, an adjective, or another adverb and tells these things:

- where: there, here, outside, inside, away
- when: now, then, later, immediately, yesterday
- how: quickly, slowly, stupidly, gracefully, effortlessly
- how often or how long: frequently, never, twice, sometimes
- how much: hardly, extremely, minimally, greatly, too, more

# Adjectives with an *-ly* tail

Most adverbs are formed by adding *-ly* to the adjective, so if you see an *-ly* word, it's usually an adverb.

| Adjective | Adverb |
|-----------|--------|
| sad | sadly |
| kind | kindly |
| quick | quickly |
| tender | tenderly |
| artistic | artistically (notice the irregular spelling: *-ally*) |
| noisy | noisily (notice the irregular spelling: *y* becomes *i*) |

# What's the big deal?

Most of the time we automatically use adverbs and adjectives correctly. In these sentences, which is correct?

> This is a (large/largely) house.
> I am (extreme/extremely) tired.
> He looked (stupid/stupidly) in that outfit.

No problem—right? Well, sometimes it's not so easy. Check this out:

**WRONG:**
> This sentence is written awful bad.
> (How is this sentence written? The question how implies that an adverb is needed, but *bad* is an adjective. *Badly* is an adverb.)

**STILL WRONG:**
> This sentence is written awful badly.
> (How badly? How implies that another adverb is needed, but *awful* is an adjective.)

**RIGHT:**
> This sentence is not written awfully badly—it's perfect!

You can get away with a lot of goofs in everyday speech, but when you are writing a paper or giving a speech, adverb and adjective goofs make your work look sloppy. Can you see what's wrong with each of these sentences?

> Meg looks real good in her new dress.
> Syman turned the corner too quick and crashed his bike.
> I made an A on the exam so easy that my mom thinks I cheated.
> Josh played awesome in the tennis match.
> I want to get my driver's license so bad I could scream.

If you can't see what's wrong with these sentences, read on. Soon you will.

## Some very common adjective and adverb goofs

| Adjective | Adverb |
| --- | --- |
| bad | badly |
| real | really |
| sure | surely |
| easy | easily |
| good | well |

---

In the following examples, <u>adjectives</u> have single underlining and <u>adverbs</u> have double underlining.

---

<u>WRONG:</u>
> I am real sure that this is a real diamond, not a fake.
> (How sure? This question implies an adverb is needed: I am *really* sure. What kind of diamond? This question implies an adjective is needed: a *real* diamond.)

<u>RIGHT:</u>
> I am really sure that this is a real diamond, not a fake.

<u>WRONG:</u>
> I did good on the exam and got a good grade on my report card.

(How did I do? An adverb is needed: I did *well*.

What kind of grade? An adjective is needed: a *good* grade.)

RIGHT:

I did <u>well</u> on the exam and got a <u>good</u> grade on my report card.

WRONG:

It was an easy match, and Austin won easy.

(What kind of match? An adjective is needed: an *easy* match.

How did he win? An adverb is needed: he won *easily*.)

RIGHT:

It was an <u>easy</u> match, and Austin won <u>easily</u>.

WRONG:

This sure seems like a sure bet.

(How does it seem? An adverb is needed: it *surely* seems.

What kind of bet? An adjective is needed: a *sure* bet.)

RIGHT:

This <u>surely</u> seems like a <u>sure</u> bet.

WRONG:

Only the bad ice skaters performed bad.

(What kind of ice skaters? An adjective is needed: *bad* ice skaters.

How did they perform? An adverb is needed: they performed *badly*.)

RIGHT:

Only the <u>bad</u> ice skaters performed <u>badly</u>.

# Same word, different job

**Some words can be either adjectives or adverbs depending on how they are used.**

| Adjective telling what kind | Adverb telling how, when, or where |
|---|---|
| He played a <u>hard</u> guitar piece. | He pounded the drums <u>hard</u>. |
| I flew past a <u>high</u> tower. | I flew <u>high</u> in the sky. |
| We are <u>close</u> friends. | Sit <u>close</u> to me. |
| You're doing a <u>fine</u> job. | You are skiing <u>fine</u> since your lesson. |
| That was a <u>low</u> blow. | I stooped <u>low</u>. |
| She was in a <u>deep</u> sleep. | She dived <u>deep</u> into the water. |
| He is a <u>fair</u> player. | He's not cheating; he's playing <u>fair</u>. |
| I'm in a <u>tight</u> spot. | Sleep <u>tight</u>. |
| That's the <u>right</u> answer. | The teacher said I spelled it <u>right</u>. |
| That's the <u>wrong</u> answer. | The teacher said I spelled it <u>wrong</u>. |
| The <u>late</u> train arrives at 10:00. | I slept <u>late</u> this morning. |
| Draw a <u>straight</u> line. | Go <u>straight</u> to your room. |

To make things even more complicated, most of these adverbs have two different forms: an -ly form and a form without the -ly. Notice that sometimes these two forms have very different meanings.

| | |
|---|---|
| Robin hit Tucker <u>hard</u>. | Robin <u>hardly</u> hit Tucker. |
| Hold your head <u>high</u>. | I <u>highly</u> recommend it. |
| Becca and Emily sit <u>close</u> together. | The girls are <u>closely</u> related. |

| | |
|---|---|
| You are cooking dinner <u>fine</u>. | We need some <u>finely</u> chopped celery. |
| He dug <u>deep</u> into the earth. | He felt <u>deeply</u> happy as he dug. |
| He's playing <u>fair</u>. | He's playing <u>fairly</u> well. |
| Pull the ropes <u>tight</u>. | These ropes are <u>tightly</u> twisted. |
| The teacher said I spelled it <u>right</u>. | She praised me <u>rightly</u>. |
| The teacher said I spelled it <u>wrong</u>. | She accused me <u>wrongly</u>. |
| I've been sleeping <u>late</u>. | I haven't been sleeping <u>lately</u>. |

Some adverbs don't have an -*ly* form.

>Austin ran <u>fast</u>. It was a <u>fast</u> race. (There is no such word as *fastly*.)
>It won't be a <u>long</u> trip. I won't be gone <u>long</u>. (There is no *longly*.)
>Marshall got up <u>early</u> because he had an <u>early</u> class. (There is no *earlyly*.)

Some -*ly* words are adjectives.

| | | |
|---|---|---|
| friendly dog | lovely sunset | deadly chemicals |
| lowly job | hilly landscape | cowardly deed |
| early flight | oily rag | hourly chore |

You can't always recognize an adverb by its -*ly* tail. You can recognize it by its job in the sentence: it tells you something about a verb or another adverb, never about a noun. And it answers one of these questions: *where? when? how? how often? how long?* or *how much?*

>Reminder: In this section
><u>adjectives</u> have single underlining
>and <u>adverbs</u> have double underlining.

# Use adverbs with action verbs and adjectives with linking verbs.

## Examples of action verbs: swim, run, jump, scream, write, sleep, eat, kiss

She skates [action] <u>gracefully.</u>   He sings [action] <u>well.</u>
He leaves [action] <u>quickly.</u>       She yells [action] <u>loudly.</u>

The most common linking verb is *be* and all of its forms: *am, was, will be, have been, will have been,* etc. Notice that in these sentences the subject is being described but isn't actually doing any type of action.

Tori is [linking] <u>tired</u>.   David was [linking] <u>thirsty.</u>
Elizabeth and Katie are   Kacey and Tucker will be
 [linking] <u>tall</u>.          [linking] <u>hungry.</u>

## Some words can be either linking verbs or action verbs depending on how they are used.

taste   sound   smell   feel   get
look   turn   grow   appear   act

Chris appears [linking—the subject is being described]
 <u>happy</u>.
The airplane appears [action] <u>suddenly</u> out of the fog.

Marshall feels [linking—the subject is being described]
 <u>tired</u>.
The vet feels [action] the cat's tummy <u>carefully</u>.

A trick to tell whether the verb is action or linking (in other words, whether to use an adjective or an adverb) is to substitute the word *seems* and notice how it sounds. If it sounds okay, it's a linking verb and you need an adjective. Otherwise, it's an action verb and you need an adverb.

The hamburger meat smells (bad/badly).
 (The meat *seems* bad? Yes, that's okay, so *smell* here
  is a linking verb and needs an adjective. *Bad* is an
  adjective.)

I smelled the hamburger meat (careful/carefully) to see if it was rotten.

> (I *seem* the meat? No, that's not okay, so *smell* here is an action verb and needs an adverb. *Carefully* is an adverb.)

## Comparisons: Big—Bigger—Biggest

**Big is called the positive; bigger is called the comparative; biggest is called the superlative.**

For short adjectives and adverbs, add *-er* and *-est*.

> Mary is thin, Lisa is thinner, Katie is thinnest.
> Camilla is smart, Lavonda is smarter, Meg is smartest.
> Come soon. Come sooner. Come the soonest you can.

For longer adjectives and most adverbs, use *more* and *most*.

**ADJECTIVES:**
> I am capable. You are more capable. Maria is most capable.

**ADVERBS:**
> I eat quickly. You eat more quickly. She eats most quickly.

Or *less* and *least*.

**ADJECTIVES:**
> Marshall is willing. Eric is less willing. Of the three, Rick is least willing.

**ADVERBS:**
> David runs gracefully. Sam runs less gracefully. Of the three, Mark runs least gracefully.

Sometimes you, the writer, must decide which sounds better, the -*er* form or the *more* form. Which do you think is better?

RIGHT:
Today is cloudier than the weather forecaster predicted.
RIGHT:
Today is more cloudy than the weather forecaster predicted.

RIGHT:
Your dog is even stupider than I thought.
RIGHT:
Your dog is even more stupid than I thought.

A few adverbs don't follow the rules. These are irregular:

You sing <u>well</u>. He sings <u>better</u>. She sings <u>best</u>.
I ski <u>badly</u>. He skis <u>worse</u>. She skis <u>worst</u>.
I ran <u>far</u>. You ran <u>farther</u>. He ran <u>farthest</u>.

A few adjectives don't follow the rules. These are irregular:

Joe is a <u>good</u> athlete. Jack is a <u>better</u> athlete. Jill is the <u>best</u> athlete.
Beets are <u>bad</u>. Olives are <u>worse</u>. Brussels sprouts are <u>worst</u>.
I have <u>little</u> luck. You have <u>less</u> luck. He has the <u>least</u> luck.
I have <u>many</u> cats. You have <u>more</u> cats. She has the <u>most</u> cats.
I ate too <u>much</u> pizza. He ate <u>more</u> pizza. You ate the <u>most</u> pizza.

Comparisons can get confusing. Try to keep them as simple as possible. Check these out:

| Confusing | Clear |
| --- | --- |
| less big | smaller |
| more powerless | less powerful |
| least harmless | most harmful |
| less unable | more able |

## Some adjectives can't get any bigger or better—they are already superlative.

WRONG:

This is my firstest trip to New York.

WRONG:

This is my most first trip to New York.

RIGHT:

This is my first trip to New York.

WRONG:

I am the onliest girl on the football team.

WRONG:

I am the most only girl on the football team.

RIGHT:

I am the only girl on the football team.

WRONG:

You are the bestest friend I have.

WRONG:

You are the most best friend I have.

RIGHT:

You are the best friend I have.

WEAK:

My mom is more pregnant than your mom.

(It's not possible to be sort of pregnant.)

BETTER:

My mom's baby is due sooner than your mom's.

WEAK:

This assignment is more complete than that one.

(Either it's complete or it's not.)

BETTER:

This assignment is closer to being finished than that one.

## Be careful where you place adverbs!

WEAK:

I had *only* been asleep for ten minutes when the phone rang and woke me up.

(This sentence actually means this: I had only been asleep [I hadn't been jogging or eating or dancing—only sleeping] for ten minutes when the phone rang.)

BETTER:

I had been asleep for *only* ten minutes when the phone rang and woke me up.

NOT VERY ROMANTIC:

My darling, I *only* think about you.
(Does this mean you never *feel* anything about me?)

BETTER:

My darling, I think *only* about you.

**Notice how the placement of an adverb can change the entire meaning of the sentence.**

RIGHT:

We spent *almost* all our money playing video games; we had only $1.50 left for lunch.

RIGHT:

We *almost* spent all our money playing video games, but we saved it and bought a bunch of baseball cards instead.

# BRAIN TICKLERS
## Set # 4

Find the goofs in these sentences and correct them.

1. The dog smells badly.

2. Of the three boys, Mike runs faster.

3. You sure can eat a lot of ice cream at one sitting!

4. This is a real pretty dress.

5. Kate is much less unintelligent than Sue.

6. Apples turn badly if you let them sit out for too long.

7. This bottle of Coke is emptier than that one.

8. I only ate three slices of pizza.

9. What a nice gesture on your part to greet them so nice when they arrived.

10. Josh's mom hugged him real sweet and said, "Enough grammar exercises. Let's take a break."

(Answers are on page 64.)

# CONJUNCTION POINTERS

## What is a conjunction?

It is a word that joins words or groups of words. The two stars among conjunctions are *and* and *but*. Here are some other conjunctions: *yet, for, so, or, because.*

### Life without conjunctions:

> I would love to go out to eat with you. I would love to go out to eat with Krista. I would love to go to the movies with you. I would love to go to the movies with Krista. My mom says I can't. My mom says I might have to do my homework. My mom says I might have to clean up my room. The reason is this: I broke my curfew last weekend.

### Life with conjunctions:

> I would love to go out to eat <u>and</u> to the movies with you <u>and</u> Krista, <u>but</u> my mom says I have to <u>either</u> do my homework <u>or</u> clean up my room <u>because</u> I broke my curfew last weekend.

*51*

# Pairing up

## Correlative conjunctions are used in pairs.

either—or    neither—nor    not only—but also

WRONG:
Neither Wesley or Elizabeth got a hit in the game.
RIGHT:
Neither Wesley nor Elizabeth got a hit in the game.

WRONG:
Not only Meg but David got a part in the play.
RIGHT:
Not only Meg but also David got a part in the play.

WRONG:
Sal cannot pitch nor catch.
RIGHT:
Sal can neither pitch nor catch.
ALSO RIGHT:
Sal cannot pitch or catch.

# Beginning a sentence with a conjunction

## As a rule, don't do it.

WEAK:
I studied for the math test. But I didn't study enough.
BETTER:
I studied for the math test, but I didn't study enough.

WEAK:
I want to be a doctor when I grow up. Or maybe a tiger tamer.
BETTER:
I want to be a doctor when I grow up, or maybe a tiger tamer.

If you don't do it very often, sometimes beginning a sentence with a conjunction creates effective emphasis.

Ryan thought the noise he heard was a grizzly bear in his bedroom. And he was right!

## Comma caution

### Avoid a common goof: don't use a comma every time you see a conjunction.

- Don't use a comma when you have a compound verb (a verb that has two or more parts).

  <u>WRONG:</u>
  Tori ate a big dinner, and slept soundly all night.
  (The subject is *Tori*; the compound verb is *ate and slept*. You wouldn't write "Tori ate, and slept." Who needs the comma?)

  <u>RIGHT:</u>
  Tori ate a big dinner and slept soundly all night.

- Don't use a comma with linking conjunctions. (Here are some linking conjunctions: *if, though, whenever, because, since, while, before, when.*) Delete the comma in each of these sentences:

  <u>WRONG:</u>
  I will walk home, because my mom can't pick me up.

WRONG:
I will eat my spinach, if you'll put some butter on it.
WRONG:
I try to hide, whenever my mom serves liver for dinner.

- Don't use a comma before *and* when only two things are listed. Get rid of the comma in each of these sentences:

WRONG:
I love chocolate cake, and chocolate ice cream.
WRONG:
I want to play pro baseball, and pro football.

- When should you use commas with conjunctions? See page 81.

# Too many *and's*

Don't overuse the conjunction *and*.

RIGHT BUT BORING:
I got up early, and I finished studying. I went to school, and I took the algebra quiz. I did well, and I felt relieved. I told my dad, and he was proud of me.
MUCH BETTER:
I got up early and finished studying for the algebra quiz before I went to school. I was relieved, and my dad was very proud that I did well on the quiz.

There are many ways to avoid the dull, boring pattern of too many *and's*. This is just one way. Can you think of others?

# Too many *so's*

Kids seem to love the word *so* and use it in every other sentence. It can make your writing weak and boring, so don't overuse it. (Did you catch that?)

WEAK:
Mom asked me to help her set the table, so I did.
BETTER:
Mom asked me to help her set the table, and I did.

**WEAK:**
>Austin studied hard, so he got a good grade.

**BETTER:**
>Austin got a good grade because he studied hard.

**WEAK:**
>The doll was old and torn, so I threw it away.

**BETTER:**
>I threw away the old, torn doll.

# PREPOSITION POINTERS

## What is a preposition?

It is a word that shows how a noun or pronoun relates to another part of the sentence.

*In, on, of, by, for, with*—prepositions are unimportant little words that we don't need to pay much attention to. Right? Wrong! Check out what a big difference a little preposition can make:

>My sister is lying <u>to</u> me.
>My sister is lying <u>next</u> <u>to</u> me.

>I am swimming <u>toward</u> the shark's tummy. Oops.
>I am swimming <u>away</u> <u>from</u> the shark's tummy as fast as I can. Hurry!
>I am swimming <u>inside</u> the shark's tummy. Bummer.

## Ending a sentence

It used to be a rigid rule that you should never end a sentence with a preposition. That rule has softened over time. If you can change the order of the words so as not to end with a preposition and the sentence sounds good, do it, but if editing makes your sentence sound weird, forget it.

**OKAY:**
Notice the ease Carlos hits the ball <u>with</u>.
**BETTER:**
Notice the ease <u>with</u> <u>which</u> Carlos hits the ball.

**OKAY:**
I'm the one she's sitting next <u>to</u>.
**BETTER:**
She is sitting next <u>to</u> me.

**OKAY:**
A senator is someone most people look up <u>to</u>.
**VERY WEIRD:**
A senator is someone <u>to</u> whom most people upwardly look.
**MUCH BETTER:**
Most people look up <u>to</u> a senator.

**RIGHT:**
What time should we wake <u>up</u>?
(In this sentence, *up* is actually not a preposition; it's part of the verb *to wake up*. Here are some other "double" verbs that sound as if they end in a preposition: to sleep over, to lie down, to throw up, to shut down, to shut up, to shut out, to burn up, to burn down.)

# Too much of a good thing

## Don't use a bunch of prepositional phrases in a row.

**AWKWARD:**
I went to a store in a town in Ohio in the middle of a flood in June, which is during Ohio's rainy season, and in a matter of minutes found myself knee-deep in water.

Did you count all ten prepositional phrases? In each phrase, the preposition is underlined:

| | | |
|---|---|---|
| <u>to</u> a store | <u>in</u> a town | <u>in</u> Ohio |
| <u>in</u> the middle | <u>of</u> a flood | <u>in</u> June |
| <u>during</u> Ohio's rainy season | <u>in</u> a matter | |
| <u>of</u> minutes | <u>in</u> water | |

<u>BETTER:</u>

Last June I visited a small Ohio town during the rainy season. When I went into a flooded store, I quickly found myself knee-deep in water.

Now we're down to only three prepositional phrases:

<u>during</u> the rainy season
<u>into</u> a flooded store
<u>in</u> water

# INTERJECTION POINTERS

## What is an interjection?

It is a little word that does these things:

- expresses a feeling: wow, gee, golly, oops, zowie, darn
- says yes or no: yes, no, yep, nope, uh-huh, uh-uh
- calls attention: yo, hey, whoa
- indicates a pause: well, um, hmm, ah

## Standing alone

If an interjection expresses a really strong feeling, it can stand alone even though it's not a complete sentence. (What is a complete sentence? See page 70.) These sentence fragments are okay:

<u>Wow</u>! That's a gorgeous dress!
<u>Ouch</u>! That hurts.

# BRAIN TICKLERS
## Set # 5

Find the goofs in these sentences and correct them.

1. I want new rollerblades. And I want a new game for the computer for my birthday.

2. Kate ate a plate of spaghetti, and a salad.

3. Meg got dressed and headed out for her horseback lesson and got there early and she groomed her horse slowly.

4. Neither Tina or Brian was able to go with us to the game.

5. Which movie are you going to?

6. We drove in our new car in a hard rain through an open field over an old bridge to the house in the country where my grandmother lives.

7. Whoa, slow down, Princess, you're galloping too fast!

(Answers are on page 65.)

# BRAIN TICKLERS— THE ANSWERS

## Set # 1, page 14

1. This is an amazing natural phenomena.

   And this is one of those tricky foreign words. *Phenomena* is plural; *phenomenon* is singular. Both of these are correct:
   • This is an amazing natural <u>phenomenon</u>.
   • These are amazing natural <u>phenomena</u>.

2. Parker is captain of the girl's softball team.

   *Girl's* is singular, so this sentence actually means that there is only one girl on the team. I'll bet you mean this: Parker is captain of the <u>girls'</u> softball team.

3. The womans' dress is made of silk.

   There is no such word as *womans'*. Both of these are correct:
   • The <u>woman's</u> dress is made of silk.
   • The <u>women's</u> dresses are made of silk.

4. Marshall and David's fingers were nearly frostbitten after playing in the snow for three hours.

   *Marshall and David's fingers* implies that Marshall and David share a set of fingers. It could also imply that Marshall's whole body was nearly frostbitten and David's fingers were nearly frostbitten. This is correct: <u>Marshall's and David's</u> fingers were nearly frostbitten after playing in the snow for three hours.

5. I asked dad to drive me to Emily's house.

   Capitalize *Father* or *Dad* when you're calling his name or referring to him without the word *my*. Both of these are correct:
   • I asked <u>my</u> dad to drive me to Emily's house.
   • I asked <u>Dad</u> to drive me to Emily's house.

6. I really Really want to go to the Brand New Mall and see whether they sell Neat Stuff!

   This sentence fell hard into the Cap Trap! Only the first word in this sentence deserves a capital letter.

7. I heard the babie's cries.

   There is no such word as *babie's*.
   - If you mean one baby making one sound: I heard the baby's cry.
   - If you mean one baby making many sounds: I heard the baby's cries.
   - If you mean two or more babies: I heard the babies' cries.

8. I borrowed my bosses car for an hour because mine was in the shop.

   *Bosses* is plural, not possessive. Nouns need apostrophes to show ownership. I borrowed my boss's car for an hour because mine was in the shop.

9. I grew up in the south.

   Major regions of the United States are capitalized. I grew up in the South.

10. The City where Batman lives is Gotham City.

    The word *city* is capitalized only when it's part of a specific town's name. The city where Batman lives is Gotham City.

## Set # 2, page 22

1. Susan remembered to bring Mary's jacket to school but forgot her gloves.

   Whose gloves—Susan's or Mary's? The antecedent is unclear. Try this: Susan remembered to bring Mary's jacket to school but forgot to bring her own gloves.

2. They don't allow kids to throw jello at each other in the cafeteria.

   In this case, it's pretty clear who *they* are—anybody nearby! As a rule, don't use the vague *they*. Let your reader know whom you're talking about. The teachers don't allow kids to throw jello at each other in the cafeteria.

3. When doing a plié, the ballerina should keep her knees over her toes. You shouldn't allow your knees to turn inward or one could damage one's knees and ankles.

   Ballerina—you—one: which is it? Be consistent. When doing a plié, the ballerina should keep her knees over her toes. She shouldn't allow her knees to turn inward or she could damage her knees and ankles.

4. I gave Todd a new bike and a video game; it made him happy.

   The antecedent is unclear. What is *it*? The bike? the video game? my kindness? Try this: I gave Todd a new bike and a video game; the birthday gifts made him happy.

5. Hello. You want to speak to Marianne? This is her.

   Would you say "her is this"? No. This is she.

6. We had a great time at Myrtle Beach; they have so much to do there.

   There's that sneaky *they*. Who are *they*? We had a great time at Myrtle Beach; there is so much to do there.

7. The teacher told we kids to be quiet.

   Would you say "the teacher told we to be quiet"? No. The teacher told us kids to be quiet.

8. We're going out to dinner alone—just Erica and me.

   Turn it around: Erica and me are going out to dinner. That's no good. It should be this: We're going out to dinner alone—just Erica and I.

9. It was him who ate all the nachos.

   Would you say "him was it"? No. It was <u>he</u> who ate all the nachos.

10. Mom gave both of us, Elizabeth and I, money for the movie.

    Turn it around: Mom gave I and Elizabeth money for the movie. That won't fly. It should be this: Mom gave both of us, Elizabeth and <u>me</u>, money for the movie.

11. Tucker is a friend of Miranda's and me.

    Would you say "Tucker is a friend of me"? No. Tucker is a friend of Miranda's and <u>mine</u>.

## Set # 3, page 39

1. Mom fusses a lot about me trashing my room.

   Remember gerunds? *Trashing* is one of them and it takes a possessive noun or pronoun. Mom fusses a lot about <u>my</u> trashing my room.

2. When I was a kid, I swang every day on an old tire my dad hanged in a tree for me.

   There are two irregular verbs in this sentence. This is correct: When I was a kid, I <u>swung</u> every day on an old tire my dad <u>hung</u> in a tree for me.

3. I wish I'd waken up earlier.

   You have two choices: waked or woken—but not waken.

4. Adam breaks the dish when he tossed it to Omar who is standing at the sink.

   Too many different verb tenses. *Breaks* is present tense, *tossed* is past tense, *is standing* is present progressive tense, and after reading this sentence, your reader is very tense! Try this: Adam <u>broke</u> [past tense] the dish when he tossed [past tense] it to Omar who <u>was</u> <u>standing</u> [past progressive tense] at the sink.

5. If I was you, I'd buy that gorgeous dress.

The word *if* is one clue that a sentence might fit the subjunctive mood, and this one does. If I <u>were</u> you, I'd buy that gorgeous dress.

6. I've laid awake all night worrying about my math test.

As you laid, did you produce any eggs? You could scramble them for breakfast or . . . oh, I bet you meant to say this: I've <u>lain</u> awake all night worrying about my math test.

7. I worked for three hours, and finally the assignment was completed.

Keep scratching your head. Can you see the goof? This sentence switches from active voice (*I worked*) to passive voice (*the assignment was completed*). It's not technically wrong, but in this case it's weak. This is better: I worked for three hours, and finally I finished the assignment.

8. My mom screamed, "I can't stand you splitting infinitives!"

Tricked you, didn't I? This goof has nothing to do with split infinitives; it has to do with gerunds. My mom screamed, "I can't stand <u>your</u> splitting infinitives!"

9. If you want to really, truly, without a doubt thrill your teacher, don't split infinitives.

There is a very badly split infinitive (*to thrill*) in this sentence. Here's a possible solution: If you really want <u>to thrill</u> your teacher, don't split infinitives.

10. The headline read, "Local Kid Won Scholarship from Pizza Hut."

This is okay, but headlines usually use the present tense for emphasis. "Local Kid <u>Wins</u> Scholarship from Pizza Hut."

## Set # 4, page 50

1. The dog smells badly.

   This might be correct—it depends on what you mean.
   - If the dog stinks: The dog smells [linking verb] <u>bad</u> [adjective].
   - If the dog has a poor sense of smell: The dog smells [action verb] <u>badly</u> [adverb].

2. Of the three boys, Mike runs faster.

   When there are three or more involved, use the superlative form. Of the three boys, Mike runs <u>fastest</u>.

3. You sure can eat a lot of ice cream at one sitting!

   How can you eat? An adverb is needed, but *sure* is an adjective. You <u>surely</u> can eat a lot of ice cream at one sitting!

4. This is a real pretty dress.

   How pretty is the dress? An adverb is needed, but *real* is an adjective. This is a <u>really</u> pretty dress.

5. Kate is much less unintelligent than Sue.

   This is correct but very confusing. This is clear: Kate is much more intelligent than Sue.

6. Apples turn badly if you let them sit out for too long.

   Could you say that apples *seem* bad? Yes, so *turn* is a linking verb here, and it needs an adjective. Apples turn <u>bad</u> if you let them sit out for too long.

7. This bottle of Coke is emptier than that one.

   This is not a problem in conversation (your listener knows what you mean) or in informal writing, but it is a problem in formal writing. Either the bottle is empty or it isn't. Both of these are correct:

- This bottle of Coke is more nearly empty than that one.
- This bottle has less Coke in it than that one.

8. I only ate three slices of pizza.

   I'm glad you only ate them. It would be a little weird if you shot baskets with them or wore those slices of pizza around your head to keep your ears warm. Oh, wait a minute, I'll bet you mean this: I ate <u>only</u> <u>three</u> slices of pizza.

9. What a nice gesture on your part to greet them so nice when they arrived.

   What kind of gesture? An adjective is needed: a nice gesture. How did you greet them? An adverb is needed: so nicely. This is correct: What a <u>nice</u> gesture on your part to greet them so <u>nicely</u> when they arrived.

10. Josh's mom hugged him real sweet and said, "Enough grammar exercises. Let's take a break."

    We can't take a break quite yet. Two adjectives sneaked into this sentence when two adverbs are needed. How did she hug him? Sweetly. How sweetly? Really sweetly. Josh's mom hugged him <u>really</u> <u>sweetly</u> and said, "Enough grammar exercises. Let's take a break."

# Set # 5, page 58

1. I want new rollerblades. And I want a new game for the computer for my birthday.

   Begin a sentence with a conjunction (*and* is a conjunction) only when you want a lot of emphasis. This is not a good place to do it. I want new rollerblades and a new game for the computer for my birthday.

2. Kate ate a plate of spaghetti, and a salad.

   Don't use a comma every time you see the word *and*. Kate ate a plate of spaghetti and a salad.

3. Meg got dressed and headed out for her horseback lesson and got there early and she groomed her horse slowly.

   There are too many *and's* in this sentence. Try this: Meg got dressed, headed out for her horseback lesson, got there early, and groomed her horse slowly.

4. Neither Tina or Brian was able to go with us to the game.

   *Neither* needs *nor*. Neither Tina nor Brian was able to go with us to the game.

5. Which movie are you going to?

   This is okay in informal writing. In formal writing, it's better not to end a sentence with a preposition. This might sound stuffy to you, but in formal, precise writing, this is better: To which movie are you going?

6. We drove in our new car in a hard rain through an open field over an old bridge to the house in the country where my grandmother lives.

   This sentence has too many prepositional phrases in a row. There are many ways to improve it. Here's one: On a very rainy day, we drove our new car through an open field and over an old bridge until we arrived at my grandmother's country house.

7. Whoa, slow down, Princess, you're galloping too fast!

   *Whoa* is an interjection. It is also a very strong feeling, so it is okay for it to stand alone. This would be better: Whoa! Slow down, Princess, you're galloping too fast!

CHAPTER TWO

# Building and Punctuating Sentences

# MAKING SENTENCES

Words are like building blocks—we can put them together in all sorts of different ways in order to make many different kinds of sentences. When we write, it is very important to make complete sentences. It is a common goof to write incomplete sentences, which are also called sentence fragments. In this chapter we'll learn how to tell whole sentences from fragments. Then we'll learn how to punctuate those sentences.

Punctuation marks do the same thing for a sentence that road signs do for a highway. Punctuation marks tell the reader when to speed up, when to slow down, when to stop, and what to expect up the road.

We'll start our exploration of punctuation with the separators. The ultimate separator is the period. It says "STOP HERE." Imagine how confusing life would be without periods really weird is how it would be everything would run together we wouldn't know where one idea stopped and another started in all likelihood before long we'd all go completely nuts

Question marks and exclamation marks are usually periods with special missions. Wow! Isn't that exciting?

The comma is the most common separator. It says "SLOW DOWN." Without commas we wouldn't know when to pause. Sentences phrases clauses and lists become confusing disorienting and jumbled when we forget how commas should be used when they should be used and equally importantly when they shouldn't be used. Think of commas as pauses to take a breath. When we speak with other people (little breath), we often pause in order to get our meaning across (little breath), and we don't run all our words together. There are more rules and guidelines about commas than any other mark of punctuation because we use them more often than any other.

There are five other separators: colons, semicolons, parentheses, dashes, and brackets. When do you use one and when do you use another? There are a few rules (okay, okay, you don't have to beg; I'll tell you the rules [just be patient]), but often the decision comes down to choice: the writer's creative option—or the writer's rights. Did you notice all five separators in that sentence?

After the separators, we'll look at these other marks of punctuation:

| | |
|---|---|
| bullets • • • | ** asterisks ** |
| . . . ellipses . . . | // slashes // |
| "quotation marks" | hy-phens |
| a pos' tro phes | <u>underlining</u> |
| *italics* | abbrev. words |
| #% symbols &@ | 5,6 numbers 7,8 |

Lots of fun is in store! Okay, it may not be as much fun as rollerblading with your friends or munching on popcorn, but hopefully it will be painless.

# SENTENCES, FRAGMENTS, PHRASES, AND CLAUSES

How can you tell a complete sentence from an incomplete sentence? Usually your ear will tell you when a sentence is complete.

**INCOMPLETE SENTENCE:**
Two miles.
(What? Who does what for two miles? I don't get it. This is not complete.)

**INCOMPLETE SENTENCE:**
Two miles every day.
(I still don't get it. Two miles every day where? Why? Who? Tell me more.)

**INCOMPLETE SENTENCE:**
Two miles every day, rain or shine.
(I don't care about the weather! Tell me who is doing what.)

**COMPLETE SENTENCE:**
I run.

(This is a very simple sentence, but it has a subject [I] and
a verb [run]. You know what happened and who did it.)

COMPLETE SENTENCE:

I run two miles.

(Here is the same sentence with a little more information.
There's no confusion here.)

COMPLETE SENTENCE:

I run two miles every day, rain or shine.

(Here is the same sentence with even more information,
and it's still very clear.)

## A complete sentence must have a subject and a verb.

What is a verb? (For more about verbs, see page 23.) It is a
word that expresses one of two things:

- action: jump, scream, fly, run
- state of being: appear, seem, feel

What is a subject? It can be any of the following things. (In
each example, the subject is underlined.)

- The person who does the action in the sentence: <u>Josh</u>
  serves the tennis ball.
- The thing that does the action in the sentence: The <u>ball</u>
  zips through the air.
- The person being described in the sentence: <u>Josh</u> is
  happy about his powerful serve.
- The thing being described in the sentence: The <u>ball</u> is
  happy when the point is over and it can rest!

Subjects can come in many different packages. (In each example, the subject is underlined.)

- One noun as the subject: The <u>dog</u> barks.
- Two nouns as the subject (this is called a compound subject, which just means it has more than one part): The
  <u>dog and cat</u> are both making noise and keeping us awake.
- One pronoun as the subject: <u>She</u> can't sleep because of
  all the noise.

- Two pronouns as the subject (this is another type of compound subject): <u>He and she</u> are both still awake because of those noisy animals.
- A phrase: <u>Staying awake all night</u> is no fun.
- A clause: <u>What makes me mad</u> is all this noise!

Sometimes the subject "hides" from you. It's there, but you have to use your imagination.

- Run! (What do you think the subject is? It is *you*. The sentence could read *You run!* But that's not how we speak or write. We leave out the word *you*, but everybody knows it's there—hiding.)
- Eat your spinach. (When your mom or dad says this to you, you know exactly what the subject is. Who is supposed to eat the spinach? *You* are, and *you* is the hidden subject of the sentence.)

## What is the difference between a clause and a phrase?

A clause has a subject and a verb; a phrase doesn't.

<u>CLAUSE:</u>
until I turn sixteen
(This has a subject [I] and a verb [turn], but you're left dangling, aren't you? It's not a complete sentence. This is

called a dependent clause. It depends on something else
to make a complete sentence.)

COMPLETE SENTENCE:
I can't drive until I turn sixteen.
(Now we know what's going on!)

PHRASE:
my big fat mouth
(We just saw that a clause has a subject and a verb.
There's no verb here; this is called a phrase. It could be
the start of a great sentence, but it needs some help. It
needs some action.)

COMPLETE SENTENCE:
My big fat mouth got me into a bunch of trouble again.
(Now there's some action! It might not be the kind of action
you like, but it makes a very clear, complete sentence.)

Let's see how complete sentences are built.

PHRASE:
my brand new kitten
(There's no verb here—no action word. What does the
kitten do?)

DEPENDENT CLAUSE:
when I come home from school
(This has a subject [I] and a verb [come], but your ear tells
you it is not a whole sentence. What happens when you
come home from school?)

INDEPENDENT CLAUSE #1:
When I come home from school, my brand new kitten
jumps all over me.
(This is a whole, complete sentence—also called an independent clause. It is independent because it doesn't need
anything else in order to be a sentence.)

PHRASE:
my pet crow
(There's no verb here. This could be interesting, but we
need some action and some more information to know
what's going on.)

DEPENDENT CLAUSE:
whom I call Lady Bird

(We have a subject [I] and a verb [call], but this clause doesn't make a bit of sense without more information. It's dependent on the rest of the sentence to make sense.)

**PHRASE:**

flies out of her tree, lands on my shoulder, and begs for sunflower seeds

(Now we're cooking, but we're still confused. There's a lot of action [*flies*, *lands*, and *begs* are all verbs], but there's no subject—no noun or pronoun. We don't know who or what is doing all this.)

**INDEPENDENT CLAUSE #2:**

My pet crow, whom I call Lady Bird, flies out of her tree, lands on my shoulder, and begs for sunflower seeds.

(This is a whole, complete sentence.)

**INDEPENDENT CLAUSE #3:**

When I come home from school, my brand new kitten jumps all over me, and my pet crow, whom I call Lady Bird, flies out of her tree, lands on my shoulder, and begs for sunflower seeds.

(Two independent clauses are often put together. Why do we join them? To make more interesting sentences!)

## Is it a sentence or is it a fragment? Sometimes it all depends on a comma.

FRAGMENT:

Soon after Kacey fell asleep.
(This is a clause with a subject and a verb, but it's not a complete sentence.)

SENTENCE:

Soon after, Kacey fell asleep.
(This is an introductory phrase [*soon after*] followed by an independent clause.)

FRAGMENT:

Before I went shopping.
(This is a clause with a subject and a verb, but it's not a complete sentence.)

SENTENCE:

Before, I went shopping.
(This is an introductory adverb [*before*] followed by an independent clause.)

## There are three times when it is okay to use fragments.

- Fragments are sometimes used effectively for emphasis.

   Katie thought she heard a brontosaurus outside her bedroom door. She gathered her courage and slowly walked to her door. She opened it. <u>Yes</u>! In fact, things were worse than she'd feared. <u>Two of them</u>!

- Fragments are fine if you're writing informal dialogue because fragments are, in fact, a common part of our everyday speech.

   Syman asked, "<u>More fries for you</u>? I have some I
      don't want."
   "<u>Sure</u>." Marshall's hand reached for the fries.
   "<u>Full</u>?" asked Syman a few minutes later.
   Marshall pushed away the remaining food. "<u>Yep</u>. Let's go."

- Fragments are fine with some exclamations and interjections.

<u>Oh, no</u>! My pet boa constrictor just crawled into bed with
Grandma!

<u>Absolutely not</u>! You may not spray paint your sister's hair
purple, and don't ask me again.

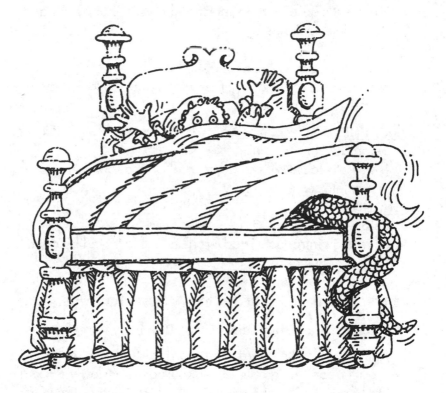

# ROAD SIGNS: PUNCTUATION

## Periods

### Use a period at the end of a complete sentence.

This rule is mighty easy.
I hope they are all this easy.

### Use periods (decimal points) with money and percentages.

$12.56          24.6%

## Use periods after initials.

My algebra teacher's name is Mr. Al G. Brough.

## Use periods in some abbreviations.

When to use periods with abbreviations can be confusing. This is an area of grammar that is changing. The trend is away from using periods. Unless you're really sure about an abbreviation, it's best to check it in a dictionary.

- Most uppercase and lowercase abbreviations still use a period.

  Months: Jan., Feb., Oct.
  Days: Mon., Tues., Wed.
  Titles: Gov., Sen., Rep., Dr., Mr., Mrs., Ms., M.D., Ph.D.
  Addresses: Ave., St., Rd., Blvd.
  Measurements: lb., oz., hr., min., ft., in., qt.
  Countries: U.S., U.K.
  Others: lat. (latitude), long. (longitude), misc. (miscella-neous), etc. (et cetera), e.g. (Latin abbreviation meaning "for example"), i.e. (Latin abbreviation meaning "in other words"), B.C. (before Christ), Inc. (incorporated)

- When all the letters are capital letters, periods are usually not used.

  Agencies, companies, and organizations: CIA, NFL, FBI, IRS, YMCA, NATO
  Computer terms: RAM, CD/ROM
  Tests: PSAT, IQ
  Radio and television stations: WQDR, KABC, ESPN
  Medical terms: AIDS, PMS
  Directions: NE, SW, NNW

- Some other common abbreviations that don't use periods:

  UFO (unidentified flying object), DST (daylight savings time), mph (miles per hour), rpm (revolutions per minute), m (meter), kg (kilogram), mg (milligram), Hz (hertz), Ca (calcium), Hg (mercury)

- Do you add a period, question mark, or exclamation mark if the sentence ends with an abbreviation that takes periods? Periods—no. Question marks and exclamation marks—yes.

<u>WRONG:</u>
Ryan woke up at 7 A.M..
<u>RIGHT:</u>
Ryan woke up at 7 A.M.
<u>WRONG:</u>
Did you wake up at 7 A.M?
<u>RIGHT:</u>
Did you wake up at 7 A.M.?
<u>WRONG:</u>
Your snoring woke me up at 2 A.M!
<u>RIGHT:</u>
Your snoring woke me up at 2 A.M.!

# Question marks

## Use a question mark after a question.

This rule is not so hard, is it?

## Use a question mark to indicate uncertainty or doubt.

The author of this book lived from 1810 (?) to 1895.
(This means you're not sure that the date 1810 is correct; perhaps no one knows for sure when this particular author was born.)

## In a polite request (when no answer is required), the question mark is often omitted even though the sentence is phrased like a question. Use it or don't use it—it is your choice.

<u>RIGHT:</u>
Would you please bring us a chocolate shake and two straws?
<u>ALSO RIGHT:</u>
Would you please bring us a chocolate shake and two straws.

## Indirect questions don't take question marks.

DIRECT QUESTION:

Is today Monday?

(This is a straight-forward question.)

INDIRECT QUESTION:

I asked whether today is Monday.

(This is a statement about a question.)

WRONG:

Josh asked whether the game was likely to be
rained out?

RIGHT:

Josh asked whether the game was likely to be
rained out.

WRONG:

I wonder whether the abominable snowman is real?

RIGHT:

I wonder whether the abominable snowman is real.

ALSO RIGHT:

Is the abominable snowman real? I wonder.

**If you have a question mark in the middle of a sentence, don't capitalize the word after the question mark.**

RIGHT:

*What in the World is a Homophone?* is a very popular children's book.

(The question mark is part of the book's title.)

RIGHT:

Will school be canceled? was on all the kids' minds.

# Exclamation points

**Use an exclamation point after exclamations. Here are some examples of exclamations:**

DELIGHT:

Wow! This is the easiest rule in the whole book!

URGENCY:

Please help me! Watch out!

ANGER:

Drop dead! Shut up!

SURPRISE:

I can't believe it's you! This is amazing!

DISTRESS:

Oh, no! This can't be happening!

EXCITEMENT:

I made straight A's on my report card!

INTENSITY:

I love you! I mean I *really* love you!

LOUD NOISES:

Bang! Crash! Boom!

STRONG COMMANDS:

Halt! Don't go one step farther!

## Is it a question or an exclamation? Sometimes a sentence can go either way.

RIGHT:

How could you do that?

ALSO RIGHT:

How could you do that!

Some people use exclamation points all the time! It makes their writing look hyperactive! Nothing looks sillier than a paragraph like this! Even worse than lots of exclamation points are—oh, no, not those!!—double exclamation points!! In formal writing, never (and I do mean *never*!!) use double exclamation points! In fact, don't use many exclamation points at all. Face it, not every sentence you write is exciting enough to deserve an exclamation point.

(See page 130 for using exclamation points with quotations. See page 103 for using exclamation points with parentheses.)

## Commas

## Use a comma before a coordinating conjunction that introduces an independent clause (that's a clause that can stand alone as a complete sentence).

Here are the coordinating conjunctions: *and, but, for, or, so, yet.*

RIGHT:

My sister's name is Miranda. My brother's name is Austin. (These are two complete, correct sentences.)

BETTER:

My sister's name is Miranda, and my brother's name is Austin.

RIGHT:

I rushed home. I finished my homework before soccer practice.

BETTER:

I rushed home, and I finished my homework before soccer practice.

WRONG:

I am very good in Spanish, and in French.

(*And in French* is not a complete sentence.)

RIGHT:

I am very good in Spanish and French.

ALSO RIGHT:

I am very good in Spanish, and I'm good in French.

(*I'm good in French* is a complete sentence.)

When the two independent clauses are very short, you have a choice:

RIGHT:

Kate slept late, but Meg got up early.

ALSO RIGHT:

Kate slept late but Meg got up early.

A comma all by itself is not strong enough to separate two independent clauses. Be alert! This is a very common comma goof.

WRONG:

We went to the beach last summer, I finally learned to wind surf.

RIGHT:

We went to the beach last summer. I finally learned to wind surf.

ALSO RIGHT:

We went to the beach last summer; I finally learned to wind surf.

ALSO RIGHT:

We went to the beach last summer, and I finally learned to wind surf.

(For when *not* to use commas with conjunctions, see page 53.)

## Use a comma after conjunctive adverbs (those are adverbs working as conjunctions—they link two sentences and show how the two are related).

Here are some conjunctive adverbs: *however, finally, furthermore, indeed, meanwhile, nevertheless, therefore, unfortunately.*

> I thought I made a C⁺ on the test; however, I made a B⁺.
> I didn't study very much; nevertheless, I made a good grade.
> I might not be so lucky next time; therefore, I'm going to study right now!

(What are those semicolons doing in these sentences? See page 98.)

## Use a comma after most introductory phrases and clauses.

> Since my mother forgot to pack me a dessert, I ate your Twinkie.
> Being a sugar freak, I have to have at least one Twinkie a day.

How do you tell what's introductory and what's not? Find the subject and verb of the sentence. Whatever comes before the subject and verb is usually an introduction.

> Since my mother forgot to pack me a dessert, I [subject] ate [verb] your Twinkie.

Don't fall for the temptation to use a comma just because the subject and verb are far apart.

**WRONG:**
> Eating too many Twinkies or other sweet things, can give you the sugar jitters.

**RIGHT:**
> Eating [subject] too many Twinkies or other sweet things can give [verb] you the sugar jitters.

When the introduction is short, you can omit the comma if you choose.

**RIGHT:**
> In June I will be going to camp.

**ALSO RIGHT:**
> In June, I will be going to camp.

But beware. What can happen if you don't use commas after introductory phrases and clauses—even short ones? Confusion, that's what!

CONFUSING:
After eating my cat
   hiccups.
(Do you eat cats often?)
CLEAR:
After eating, my cat
   hiccups.

Notice that if you reverse the order of this sentence (putting the
subject and verb first), you no
longer have an introduction and
no longer need a comma.

My cat hiccups after eating.

## Use commas to emphasize an adverb.

RIGHT:
Tori ran fast and got home before her mother.
MORE EMPHASIS:
Tori ran, fast, and got home before her mother.

RIGHT:
He fell off his bicycle hard after he skidded on loose gravel.
MORE EMPHASIS:
He fell off his bicycle, hard, after he skidded on loose gravel.

## Use commas when adjectives come after the noun.

My tennis racket, freshly strung and shiny new, will surely
   bring me good luck in the tournament.
My language arts teacher, kind of heart and generous
   of spirit, will surely give me an A if I learn all these
   comma rules.

## Use commas in lists.

RIGHT:
Please buy eggs, milk, bread, and cereal at the store.
RIGHT:
We studied math, history, health, and grammar.

**OKAY:**

> When I go on vacation, I like playing tennis and roller-
> blading and trying to beat my dad at Putt-Putt.

**MUCH BETTER:**

> When I go on vacation, I like playing tennis, rollerblading,
> and trying to beat my dad at Putt-Putt.

Is it okay to omit the last comma? Most newspapers omit it (in order to save space), but many good writers use it.

**OKAY:**

> This train goes to Norfolk, Washington, New York,
> and Boston.

**ALSO OKAY:**

> This train goes to Norfolk, Washington, New York
> and Boston.

Take your pick, but be consistent and be aware of potential problems when you don't use the final comma.

**SAY WHAT?**

> I like peanut butter and jelly, macaroni and cheese and
> bananas covered with chocolate.
> (Macaroni and cheese covered with chocolate? Yuck!)

**MUCH BETTER:**

> I like peanut butter and jelly, macaroni and cheese, and
> bananas covered with chocolate.

## Use commas with cities and states. Notice *both* commas.

> I was born in Atlanta, Georgia, on Valentine's Day.

## Use commas with addresses. Notice there is no comma between the state and the zip code.

> She lives at 225 Valley Road, Durham, North Carolina
> 27710.

## Use commas in numbers over 999.

> There were 24,567 deliriously happy fans at the
> football game.

### Use commas with direct quotations (what someone says).

"There's a big worm in my bed," yelled Miranda.
"I'm eight years old," Robin said, "and I'm in third grade."

Use commas only with direct quotations, not with indirect quotations.

DIRECT QUOTATION:
Kate said, "I want to gallop off into the sunset."
(This is a straight-forward quotation of what Kate said, using her exact words.)

INDIRECT QUOTATION:
Kate said that she wants to gallop off into the sunset.
(This is my report of what Kate said, but not necessarily using her exact words. Notice there is no comma after *Kate said*.)

WRONG:
Elizabeth said, that she wants to swim with dolphins someday.

RIGHT:
Elizabeth said that she wants to swim with dolphins someday.

(See pages 127-132 for more about punctuating quotations.)

### Use commas when speaking directly to someone (this is called direct address).

Keith, it's time to brush your teeth.
I've told you twice, boys and girls, to do your homework.

A little bitty comma can make a great big difference. Check this out:

**DIRECT ADDRESS:**
I don't want any more, honey.
**NO ADDRESS:**
I don't want any more honey.

## Use commas with dates.

**RIGHT:**
I was born on Thursday, December 27, 1979, in Boston.
(Notice all three commas. It's a very common mistake to leave out one or two.)
**ALSO RIGHT:**
I was born in December 1979, in Boston.
(When you use just the month and year, only one comma is needed.)

## Use a comma before and/or after an interjection.

(See page 57 for more about interjections.)

Wow, what a beautiful dress.
Hey, that's my lunch! No, I don't want to share my lunch with you.
Well, well, well. My goodness, you've grown so much.
I told Ryan that, yes, I'd go with him to the movies.

## Use commas between consecutive adjectives (two or more in a row) describing the same noun.

**RIGHT:**
It was a dark, cold, dreary night.
(*Dark*, *cold*, and *dreary* all describe the noun *night*.)
**ALSO RIGHT:**
It was a cold September night.
(*Cold* and *September* both describe the noun *night*, but no comma is used. When do you use a comma and when don't you? Use a comma wherever the word *and* would sound right.)

RIGHT:

I bought some expensive, stylish white tennis shoes.
- Does this sound okay: expensive *and* stylish shoes? Yes, so the comma is needed between them.
- Does this sound okay: stylish *and* white shoes? That one's iffy. It's okay to leave out the comma.
- Does this sound okay: white *and* tennis shoes? No, so don't use a comma there.

Here's another trick: use a comma when you could switch the order of the adjectives and the sentence would still sound right.

RIGHT:

I wore blue tennis shoes.
(Does this sound okay: I wore tennis blue shoes? No, so no comma is needed.)

RIGHT:

It was a dark, cold, dreary night.
(Does this sound okay: It was a cold, dark night? Yes, so the comma is needed. Does this sound okay: It was a dreary, cold night? Yes, so that comma is also needed.)

Alert! Don't put a comma before the noun.

WRONG:

I ate a beautiful, ripe, delicious, firm, apple.

RIGHT:

I ate a beautiful, ripe, delicious, firm apple.

## Use commas before and/or after some Latin abbreviations.

RIGHT:

I love sports, e.g., baseball, basketball, and football.
(*E.g.* means "for example.")

RIGHT:

A vet works with many types of animals—dogs, cats, horses, cows, etc.
(*Etc.* means "and so forth.")

## Use commas before and after parenthetical expressions.

By-the-way phrases are words inserted into a sentence giving information or thoughts that are not absolutely essential.

RIGHT:
> I reminded Mom, in case she'd forgotten, that I really want a Sega Saturn system for my birthday.

RIGHT:
> They usually cost, if you get a good deal, about $230.

RIGHT:
> Since she's the best mom in the world, or at least that's what I tell her to get her to do whatever I want, I'm sure she'll get me one.

(See page 100 for more about parenthetical expressions.)

## Use commas after greetings and before closings in friendly letters.

GREETING:
> Dear Miranda,

GREETING:
> Dear Mom,

CLOSING:
> Love,

CLOSING:
> Sincerely,

WRONG:
> Dear Governor Sutton,

RIGHT:
> Dear Governor Sutton:
> (This is not a friendly letter. It's a formal letter, and a colon should be used.)

## Use a comma to show that two parts of a sentence are being contrasted.

RIGHT:
> I ordered pizza, not lasagna.

BUILDING AND PUNCTUATING SENTENCES

I'm going out with Kevin, not Sam.

## Use commas with titles when they come after (but not before) the person's name.

Notice the commas before and after the title.

<u>RIGHT:</u>
Arith Metic, Ph.D., is my math teacher.
<u>BUT NO COMMAS HERE:</u>
Dr. Metic is my math teacher.

<u>RIGHT:</u>
Jacques Roche, D.V.M., is
a famous cockroach
veterinarian.
<u>BUT NO COMMAS HERE:</u>
Dr. Roche is a famous
cockroach veterinarian.

## Use commas before and after appositives (an appositive explains who or what the noun is).

<u>RIGHT:</u>
Our principal, John Bossman, gave a great speech.
(The subject is *principal*. The appositive, *John Bossman*,
tells more about who the subject is.)
<u>BUT NO COMMAS HERE:</u>
Principal John Bossman gave a great speech.
(In this case *John Bossman* is part of the subject. If you
leave out his name, the sentence doesn't make sense.)

<u>RIGHT:</u>
Katie Stevens, the best ballerina in the performance, shone
as the star of the evening.
(*The best ballerina in the performance* explains who Katie
Stevens is.)

BUT NO COMMAS HERE:
>> Ballerina Katie Stevens shone as the star of the evening.
>> (*Ballerina Katie Stevens* is all one unit, not one phrase
   telling more about another phrase.)

RIGHT:
>> Joshua Zinn, world-famous aardvark trainer, will be in
   town next week to demonstrate his great skills.
>> (*World-famous aardvark trainer* explains who Joshua
   Zinn is.)

BUT NO COMMAS HERE:
>> World-famous aardvark trainer Joshua Zinn will be in town
   next week to demonstrate his great skills.
>> (*World-famous aardvark trainer Joshua Zinn* is all one unit,
   not one phrase telling more about another phrase.)

## Use commas to indicate omitted words.

RIGHT:
>> I ordered chicken; Amanda, fish.
>> (This means "I ordered chicken; Amanda ordered fish.")

RIGHT:
>> Tonight I will study math; tomorrow, Spanish.
>> (This means "Tonight I will study math; tomorrow I will
   study Spanish.")

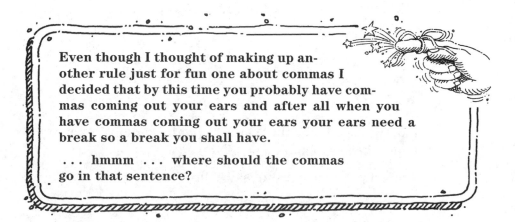

Even though I thought of making up another rule just for fun one about commas I
decided that by this time you probably have commas coming out your ears and after all when you
have commas coming out your ears your ears need a
break so a break you shall have.

... hmmm ... where should the commas
go in that sentence?

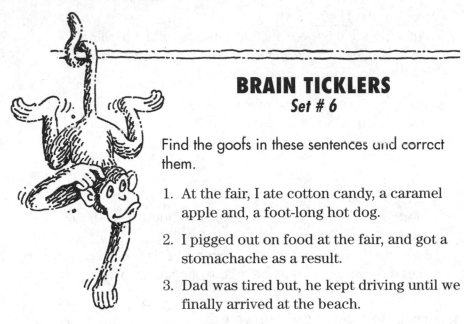

# BRAIN TICKLERS
## Set # 6

Find the goofs in these sentences and correct them.

1. At the fair, I ate cotton candy, a caramel apple and, a foot-long hot dog.

2. I pigged out on food at the fair, and got a stomachache as a result.

3. Dad was tired but, he kept driving until we finally arrived at the beach.

4. Whatever you do do it well.

5. I live in a charming, old, nineteenth-century, house.

6. Today is Wednesday December 25, 1996.

7. People from Raleigh, North Carolina often vacation at Myrtle Beach, South Carolina.

8. I admit that yes I did put that turtle in the toilet.

9. The tall guy on the basketball team Legs Long is my neighbor.

10. The new kid on the tennis team whom I beat last week won the tournament.

11. Everyone, who hasn't finished the test, must stay after school to finish it.

12. At sunset beach walks are beautiful.

13. I know I said I'd be there at 9:00, but hey I didn't count on twelve inches of snow.

14. I called you Becca just to say hello.

15. Allison bought a lacy, bright, red dress.

16. Dr Austin Stevens and Gov Hartley Hsu were at the meeting.

17. Did the package arrive c.o.d?

18. I wonder whether it's going to rain?

19. Why did you bring your math teacher a bouquet of flowers instead of bringing her your overdue homework assignment, I wondered?

20. The huge dinosaurs, creatures of the distant past, pictured on the pages of history books roaming vast plains a million years ago, with their gazing eyes and huge bodies, lumbering along with no concern for what lay in their paths, creating terror wherever they roamed.

(Answers are on page 142.)

# Colons

## Use a colon when you want to say "here comes an example" or "here's what I'm talking about."

RIGHT:
This sentence is grammatically correct: I wonder if wolves actually wolf down their pizzas the way I wolf down mine.

RIGHT:
There's one thing I love more than anything else in the world: a grammatically correct sentence.

RIGHT:
There's only one sport for me: alligator wrestling.

Notice how colons are used after the words right and wrong in this book. The colon says "here comes an example."

## Use a colon before some lists.

A colon is needed before these phrases: *these are, there are, the following, as follows, such as,* or *these things.*

RIGHT:
My favorite sports are the following: baseball, basketball, soccer, football, squash, racketball, tennis, lacrosse, golf, and every other game that's played with a ball.

<u>WRONG:</u>

The ingredients are: flour, eggs, sugar, milk, and chocolate.
(Don't use a colon if the list comes right after a verb.)

<u>RIGHT:</u>

The ingredients are flour, eggs, sugar, milk, and chocolate.

<u>ALSO RIGHT:</u>

These are the ingredients: flour, eggs, sugar, milk, and chocolate.

<u>WRONG:</u>

I want to travel to: New York, San Francisco, Atlanta, and Montreal.
(Don't use a colon if the list comes right after a preposition.)

<u>RIGHT:</u>

I want to travel to New York, San Francisco, Atlanta, and Montreal.

<u>ALSO RIGHT:</u>

I want to travel to the following cities: New York, San Francisco, Atlanta, and Montreal.

## Use a colon before subtitles of books, articles, chapters, etc.

The title of the book is *Michael Jordan: Basketball Superman.*

## Use colons with expressions of time.

It's 12:15 P.M.
His record for the mile is 4:06:27.

## Use a colon in the greeting part of a formal letter or business letter.

To Whom It May Concern:
Dear Senator Kirkpatrick:

## Use a colon in literary references between volume and page or between chapter and verse.

John 3:16 [the book of John, chapter 3, verse 16]
*Encyclopedia Brittanica* IV:425 [volume 4, page 425]

### Use a colon with ratios.

The bill passed easily; the vote was 3:1. [three to one]

### Use colons to indicate dialogue when you're writing a play or a script (and notice there are no quotation marks when you write dialogue this way).

Brian: I want to play baseball.
Mike: Great idea.
Brian: I'll get my gear and you get yours.
Mike: Meet you at the field.

### Use a colon before a long, formal quotation.

Governor Smith stated to the press: "I think that children should study grammar for at least six hours a day. Learning to speak and write correctly is far more important than anything else—including eating. In fact, I believe that eating is a complete waste of valuable time. And that is why I'm suggesting that lunch period be canceled and that students study grammar instead of eating while they are at school."

Fortunately, Governor Smith then said, "April Fools'!"

### Use a colon after words such as *caution, wanted,* or *note.*

Caution: slippery floor
Wanted: part-time waitresses and waiters
Note: We're almost finished with colons!

### Capitalize the first word after a colon if it begins a complete sentence—and if you want to. Either way is okay; it's your choice.

<u>WRONG:</u>
These are the ingredients: Apples, olives, sugar, onions, artichokes, and chocolate. Sounds yummy, doesn't it?
(*Apples* does not begin a complete sentence.)

<u>RIGHT:</u>

These are the ingredients: apples, olives, sugar, onions, artichokes, and chocolate. Sounds yummy, doesn't it?

<u>RIGHT:</u>

I'm sure you know the old saying about apples: An apple a day keeps the doctor away.

(*An* begins a complete sentence.)

<u>ALSO RIGHT:</u>

I'm sure you know the old saying about apples: an apple a day keeps the doctor away.

# Semicolons

## Use a semicolon between two sentences that are very closely related.

<u>RIGHT:</u>

My family is Jewish. We celebrate Chanukah but not Christmas.

<u>BETTER:</u>

My family is Jewish; we celebrate Chanukah but not Christmas.

(Being Jewish and celebrating Chanukah are very closely related, and that relationship is emphasized by putting them in the same sentence.)

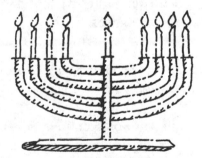

<u>WRONG:</u>

My family is Jewish; not Christian.

(*Not Christian* is not a complete sentence. Use a semicolon only between two complete sentences.)

<u>RIGHT:</u>

My family is Jewish, not Christian.

RIGHT:

My dad is a coach at the university. We get free tickets to any sports event we want to see.
(These two sentences are very closely related.)

BETTER:

My dad is a coach at the university; we get free tickets to any sports event we want to see.

WRONG:

My dad is a coach at the university; we have some cousins who live in Texas.
(Being a coach and having cousins in Texas are not closely related.)

RIGHT:

My dad is a coach at the university. We have some cousins who live in Texas.

WRONG:

I have three dogs; and two of them are golden retrievers.
(When you use a semicolon, don't use a conjunction.)

RIGHT:

I have three dogs; two of them are golden retrievers.

ALSO RIGHT:

I have three dogs, and two of them are golden retrievers.

## Use a semicolon before *however* and similar words (these words are called conjunctive adverbs) that show a relationship between two complete sentences.

WRONG:

I bet you thought you wouldn't have to learn another semi-colon rule, however, you were wrong.

RIGHT:

I bet you thought you wouldn't have to learn another semi-colon rule; however, you were wrong.

ALSO RIGHT:

I bet you thought you wouldn't have to learn another semi-colon rule. However, you were wrong.

Here are some other conjunctive adverbs: *also, besides, indeed, otherwise, therefore, in fact, meanwhile, in addition, consequently, nevertheless, next, still, finally, earlier, naturally, certainly.*

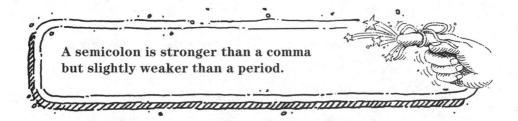

**A semicolon is stronger than a comma but slightly weaker than a period.**

## Use semicolons between clauses or phrases that contain a lot of commas.

<u>CONFUSING:</u>
> Wesley likes books about baseball, biplanes, and bagels, Brian likes books about antique cars, blimps, and rare fish, and Tori likes books about racehorses, dolls, and military jets.

<u>BETTER:</u>
> Wesley likes books about baseball, biplanes, and bagels; Brian likes books about antique cars, blimps, and rare fish; and Tori likes books about racehorses, dolls, and military jets.

<u>CONFUSING:</u>
> We saw Meg, captain of the basketball team, Marshall, captain of the tennis team, Syman, captain of the crew, and Lisa, captain of the volleyball team.

<u>BETTER:</u>
> We saw Meg, captain of the basketball team; Marshall, captain of the tennis team; Syman, captain of the crew; and Lisa, captain of the volleyball team.

<u>ALSO GOOD:</u>
> We saw Meg (captain of the basketball team), Marshall (captain of the tennis team), Syman (captain of the crew), and Lisa (captain of the volleyball team).

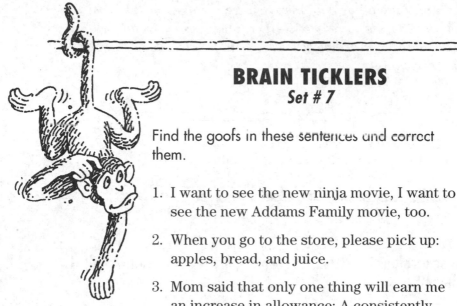

## BRAIN TICKLERS
### Set # 7

Find the goofs in these sentences and correct them.

1. I want to see the new ninja movie, I want to see the new Addams Family movie, too.

2. When you go to the store, please pick up: apples, bread, and juice.

3. Mom said that only one thing will earn me an increase in allowance: A consistently clean room.

4. I love the colors green, blue, and red, the names Vanessa, Charlotte, and Cassandra, the states Iowa, Idaho, and Illinois, but not the foods anchovies, olives, and eggplant.

5. I was on the swim team last year, we had a winning season.

6. I like chocolate cake; my dad cooks great spaghetti.

7. This is the weather report for tomorrow, heavy rain, gusty winds, and a chance of flooding.

8. I hoped it would snow, finally, it did.

(Answers are on page 145.)

# Parentheses

### Use parentheses to set off parenthetical expressions from the main part of the sentence.

What is a parenthetical expression? It is by-the-way information (inserted in the middle of a sentence, like this) that isn't absolutely necessary. Notice in all the following examples that you could leave out the parenthetical information and the sentence would still make sense, but if you want to include it, you can "tuck it in" inside parentheses. Here are some examples of parenthetical expressions:

- An explanation: The academic year (this year that's August 20-June 13) includes 180 school days.
- A translation: I paid 40 German marks (about $25) for dinner.
- A clarification: The town where I live (Chapel Hill) is in the central part of North Carolina.
- A feeling: School is canceled (yippee!) today.
- A joke or play on words: We're having chocolate mousse (no, not chocolate *moose*) for dessert.
- An opinion: We're all out (and I hope we'll remain out) of livermush.
- A list: Some of my cousins (Bill, Kristen, David, Robin, Melissa, and Kacey) were at my party.

### Don't use parentheses to ramble and throw everything except the kitchen sink into your sentence.

LOUSY WRITING:

My next-door neighbor (her name is Tori, just like my cousin) bought a new car (I think it's a Mazda, but I'm not sure; I like Mazdas) last week (on Friday, the day right after my birthday, in fact) and took me for a ride to Erica's house (she was getting ready for her trip to Arizona) right after she got home (Tori had had a long day at work) with it (the car, I mean—not the long day at work!).

### Punctuating sentences with parentheses can sometimes be tricky.

Notice the correct position of the comma or period in these sentences.

WRONG:

When I'm hungry (like now,) all I can think about is food.

WRONG:

When I'm hungry, (like now) all I can think about is food.

RIGHT:

When I'm hungry (like now), all I can think about is food.

WRONG:

I took my girlfriend out to dinner (if you can call splitting a hot dog dinner.)

RIGHT:

I took my girlfriend out to dinner (if you can call splitting a hot dog dinner).

WRONG:

Don't pay attention to Sam. (He doesn't know what he's talking about). Pay attention to me.

RIGHT:

Don't pay attention to Sam. (He doesn't know what he's talking about.) Pay attention to me.

(If a complete sentence falls inside the parentheses, put the period inside.)

RIGHT:

> Don't pay attention to Sam (he doesn't know what he's talking about); pay attention to me.
>
> (Even though the parenthetical comment is a complete sentence, I've chosen to embed it in a larger sentence. Notice the correct punctuation—no capital letter to begin it and no period.)

## Here are a few more examples of punctuating with parentheses.

Notice carefully where periods, commas, question marks, and exclamation marks belong.

> I'm angry (really angry!) about your going to the movie without me.
>
> (Only the parenthetical comment is an exclamation.)

> We loved the movie (it's great!).
>
> (Only the parenthetical comment is an exclamation. In this example, notice the order: exclamation mark, parenthesis, period.)

> What an exciting movie (*Cliffhanger*)!
>
> (In this case, the whole sentence is an exclamation.)

> I'm sad (that doesn't surprise you, does it?) about your going to the movie without me.
>
> (Only the parenthetical comment is a question.)

> Did you enjoy the movie (did you stay awake through it?)?
>
> (Both the parenthetical comment and the whole sentence are questions. This punctuation looks odd, but it's correct.)

> I'm sad about your going to the movie without me. (Promise you won't do it again?)
>
> (The parenthetical comment is a whole sentence and is not embedded in a larger sentence. Punctuate it as you would any other sentence.)

> I'm sad about your going to the movie without me (promise you won't do it again?) because I really wanted to see it.

(The parenthetical comment is a whole sentence, but this time it is embedded in a larger sentence. Don't use a capital letter to begin it unless the first word is a word that must always be capitalized; for example, *Elizabeth* or *Santa Claus*.)

I'm sad about your going to the movie without me (please don't do it again) because I really wanted to see it

Notice that when you embed a whole sentence in another sentence, if it's a question, you use the question mark. If it's an exclamation, you use the exclamation mark. If it's a statement, do not use the period.

RIGHT:
I'm happy (are you?) that there's no school today.

RIGHT:
I'm happy (ecstatic is more like it!) that tomorrow is my birthday.

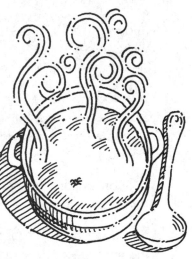

RIGHT:
I'm happy (you are probably miserable) that an itsy bitsy spider is swimming in your soup.

# Brackets

**Use brackets to insert one parenthetical comment inside another parenthetical comment.**

It is usually better, however, to rewrite sentences with too many parenthetical comments.

RIGHT:
My new mountain bike (which cost me $500 [my entire savings!]) weighs only 23 pounds.

BETTER:
My new mountain bike cost me $500 (my entire savings!) and weighs only 23 pounds.

RIGHT:
My mom (she's 35 years old [her twin sisters are 28 years old]) is the oldest kid in her family.

BETTER:
My mom is the oldest kid in her family; she is 35 years old and her twin sisters are 28 years old.

## Use brackets to insert explanations or instructions that are not actually part of the sentence.

The correct way to write the sentence is this: Each [singular subject] of the boys is [singular verb] here.

## Use brackets to insert your own editorial comments into quoted material.

The brackets say "these are my words, not the quoted person's words."

- Use brackets for clarity.

  Mike said, "We all want Z-man [Joshua Zinn] to go to the baseball card show with us this weekend."
  (Here the writer is telling the reader that when Mike speaks about Z-man, he is referring to Joshua Zinn. Mike didn't say "Joshua Zinn," the writer is adding the information for clarity.)

- Use brackets to indicate that you're unsure about something the quoted person is saying.

  The young man said, "I was born in 1930 [?] in Ohio."
  (Here the writer is not sure the young man was correct in giving his birth date as 1930. How could he be young if he were born in 1930?)

- A writer or editor uses brackets to point out an error. The sign he or she uses is [sic]. It means "the person I'm quoting made the goof, not me."

  The principal said, "Everybody in our school—all 50 [sic] of us—wants to see a big victory at Friday [sic] night's football game."
  (The writer or editor knows that there are 500—not 50—students in the school and that the ball game is on

Saturday night, not Friday. The writer is quoting the principal correctly, using his or her exact words, but is also pointing out the goofs in what the principal said.)

# Dashes

## Use a dash to link two parts of a sentence.

Dashes add emphasis—a bit of dash, you might say—and often make sentences stronger or more interesting than conjunctions do.

OKAY:
Always hook your seat belt because it's the law.
STRONGER:
Always hook your seat belt—it's the law.

OKAY:
I gave you my last $20, so don't waste it.
STRONGER:
I gave you my last $20—don't waste it.

## Use dashes to emphasize by-the-way, parenthetical expressions.

My grandmother bought me a puppy—an adorable little bulldog!—for my birthday.
I've lived in Portland—the one in Oregon, not Maine—all my life.

## Use a dash for clarity and emphasis.

### CONFUSING AND WEAK:
Finally Robin fell exhausted into bed on top of the cat.
### CLEAR AND STRONG:
Finally Robin fell exhausted into bed—on top of the cat!


## Use a dash to set off a long appositive (a description of who or what the subject is) or an appositive with lots of commas.

### RIGHT:
I love Beaver Creek, a small ski area in Colorado with long, challenging runs.
### BETTER:
I love Beaver Creek—a small ski area in Colorado with long, challenging runs.

### RIGHT:
Beautiful fish swam close to us, the colorful kinds of fish you might see in a pet store.
### BETTER:
Beautiful fish swam close to us—the colorful kinds of fish you might see in a pet store.

### CLEAR:
My best friend, Mike, is here.
### CONFUSING:
My best friends, Mike, Kevin, Brian, and Paul, are here.
### BETTER:
My best friends—Mike, Kevin, Brian, and Paul—are here.
### ALSO GOOD:
My best friends (Mike, Kevin, Brian, and Paul) are here.


## Use a dash in dialogue to show hesitation or a break in the flow of the sentence.

Parker said, "I definitely studied enough for the test—or I think I studied enough—I probably studied nearly enough—well, I hope I studied enough."

## Use a dash to sum up a list or idea.

> Red, white, and blue—those are the American colors.
> Victory—that's the name of the game.

Some writers think dashes indicate sloppy writing—no way! Dashes are energetic marks of punctuation—they can show excitement or surprise—they're spunky and lively. However, if you use too many of them—as I've done here—your writing looks like it's covered with snail tracks—not to mention chopped up and foolish. Pick your spots for dashes carefully—don't overdo it.

---

Some writers make dashes with no space before or after—like this. Others prefer to leave one space before and after dashes — like this. If you are typing on a typewriter or on a computer that won't make a dash, use two hyphens -- like this.

---

# Parenthetical (by-the-way) expressions
## Should you use parentheses, commas, or dashes?

Think of parentheses as hiding information (de-emphasizing it) while dashes highlight information—emphasizing it. Think of commas as being matter-of-fact, neither highlighting nor hiding information. If the parenthetical information is very closely related to the sentence, commas are usually better. If the parenthetical information is not so closely related, dashes and parentheses are usually better. Notice the subtle differences in these sentences. In each case, I prefer the third example, but all of these sentences are correct. Which do you prefer?

> The tennis team (especially Jim) played great.
> The tennis team, especially Jim, played great.
> The tennis team—especially Jim—played great.

The tennis team, except for Matt, played great.
The tennis team—except for Matt—played great.
The tennis team (except for Matt) played great.

Erica looked beautiful, incredibly beautiful, in her
  prom gown.
Erica looked beautiful (incredibly beautiful) in her
  prom gown.
Erica looked beautiful—incredibly beautiful—in her
  prom gown.

If you eat too much ice cream (as I've done today), you'll
  get fat.
If you eat too much ice cream—as I've done today—you'll
  get fat.
If you eat too much ice cream, as I've done today, you'll
  get fat.

# BRAIN TICKLERS
## Set # 8

Find the goofs in these sentences and correct
them.

1. Don't even think of trying to buy beer (It's
   against the law.) before you're 21 years old.

2. It is dangerous (potentially deadly)! to drink
   and drive.

3. There is only one thing I need to be happy
   (or I should say *really* happy:) chocolate.

4. I am excited (really excited!) about the party.

5. I want three things for Christmas, video games, rollerblades,
   and baseball cards.

(Answers are on page 147.)

109

# Hyphens

## Use hyphens in some compound words (two or more separate words that we think of as one unit).

Be careful—this is tricky territory! There's no absolute rule for when to use one word, two words, or a hyphen, so check your dictionary.

Is it cheerleader, cheer leader, or cheer-leader?

Is it president-elect, president elect, or presidentelect?

Is it spring break, springbreak, or spring-break?

Is it self-awareness, self awareness, or selfawareness?

Is it baby talk, babytalk, or baby-talk?

(In all five examples, the first spelling is correct.)

Is it *vice-president* or *vice president*? Both are correct. Is it *X ray* or *X-ray*? Both are correct. Sometimes you can be right either way—sometimes not even all dictionaries agree whether to use a hyphen. Choose a good dictionary and trust it. And be consistent; if you use the spelling *vice-president* in one place, use the same spelling throughout your paper.

## Use a hyphen with some prefixes, especially *all-, co-, ex-, half-, great-*, numbers, and capital letters.

all-knowing, all-around
co-conspirator, co-author
ex-husband, ex-convict
half-truth, half-hearted
great-grandmother, great-uncle
5-cent piece of candy, 40-foot tree
T-shirt, PG-rated

## Use a hyphen when a word would be confusing or hard to read without it.

CONFUSING:
shelllike (three *l*'s in a row)
CLEAR:
shell-like

CONFUSING:
Anne recovered from the flu and recovered her living
room chair.
CLEAR:
Anne recovered from the flu and re-covered her living
room chair.

CONFUSING:
The teacher remarked that he needed to remark the exams.
CLEAR:
The teacher remarked that he needed to re-mark the exams.

## Use a hyphen with double last names.

Mary Scott-Simons
Jim Blake-Adams

## Use hyphens with words that are meant to be read as a single unit.

the Braves-Mets game

the Stevens-Hsu-Sutton-Elliott family reunion
the Atlanta-Boston flight

## Use hyphens (or slashes) with dates.

RIGHT:
12-27-79
ALSO RIGHT:
12/27/79

## Use a hyphen with compound numbers from 21 to 99.

twenty-two    thirty-five
sixty-six     one hundred and sixty-two

## Use a hyphen with fractions acting as adjectives or adverbs, but not fractions acting as nouns.

RIGHT:
The bottle of Coke was two-thirds [adverb] full.
RIGHT:
Jill drank two thirds [noun] of the bottle of Coke.

## Use a hyphen with scores.

We beat our arch rivals 86-78.

## Use hyphens in compound adjectives if they come before the noun they describe.

(A compound adjective is two or more words that belong together and should be read as one word.)

the 15-year-old girl
up-to-date technology
eighth-grade students
a drive-me-completely-nuts class

If the compound adjective comes after the noun, don't use
hyphens.

The girl is 15 years old.
The technology is up to date.

The students are eighth graders.
This class is going to drive me completely nuts.

Be careful—some words that look like compound adjectives aren't.

WRONG:
Miranda is a healthy-happy girl.
(These are two separate, independent adjectives. Either could be used alone and the sentence would make sense.)

RIGHT:
Miranda is a healthy, happy girl.

WRONG:
Baseball is a frequently-played sport.
(*Frequently* is an adverb describing *played*, not part of a compound adjective.)

RIGHT:
Baseball is a frequently played sport.

Sometimes a little hyphen can make a huge difference.

CONFUSING:
The second hand painted doll sold for $50.

DO YOU MEAN:
The second-hand painted doll sold for $50?

OR DO YOU MEAN:
The second hand-painted doll sold for $50?

## Use a hyphen to mean *through.*

Read pages 16-24 before class tomorrow.
The baseball card store is open Monday-Saturday.
William Shakespeare (1564-1616) is perhaps the most famous writer of all time.

In formal writing, it is usually better to write out the word *through.*

INFORMAL:
I remained in Florida Monday-Thursday.

FORMAL:
I remained in Florida from Monday through Thursday.

## Use hyphens to spell out words.

She said, "My name is Kacey, K-a-c-e-y."

## Use hyphens to show faltering speech.

Oh, no! Y-y-you t-t-took my pl-pl-plums!

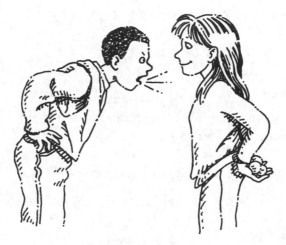

## Use hyphens for hyphenating words.

Hyphenation is important when you're writing in narrow columns (for example, a newspaper article) and need to divide words. Most of the time when you're writing by hand or on a computer, there's no need to hyphenate. When you do hy-phen-ate, you must break the word prop-er-ly. If you are un-sure where a word breaks, look it up in your dic-tion-ary.

> This is a hyphen-
> This is a dash—
> This is okay as a dash--

# Apostrophes

## Use an apostrophe with nouns to indicate ownership.

(See page 7 for more on making nouns possessive.)

| | | |
|---|---|---|
| Robin's baseball | Marshall's racket | my sister's cat |
| the Harrises' car | the Joneses' house | the women's dresses |

But don't use an apostrophe with possessive pronouns (pronouns that show ownership).

WRONG:
This house is their's.
RIGHT:
This house is theirs.

WRONG:
Is this bat your's?
RIGHT:
Is this bat yours?

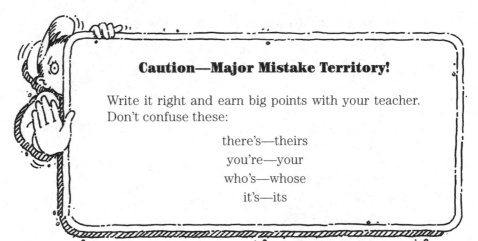

### Caution—Major Mistake Territory!

Write it right and earn big points with your teacher. Don't confuse these:

there's—theirs
you're—your
who's—whose
it's—its

WRONG:
When your writing a paper, its very important to use these words correctly. Whose going to take you're writing seriously if theirs a goof in every sentence?

**RIGHT:**

> When you're writing a paper, it's very important to use these words correctly. Who's going to take your writing seriously if there's a goof in every sentence?

## Use an apostrophe to indicate missing letters.

| | |
|---|---|
| 10 of the clock = 10 o'clock | I like them = I like 'em |
| 1993 = '93 | it is = it's |
| we were not = we weren't | you are = you're |

If you use *y'all* or *ain't* in informal writing, put the apostrophes in the right places.

**WRONG:**

> I absolutely hate it when folks from up north spell *y'all* "ya'll"! I know you true-blooded Southerners a'int never gonna spell it thataways.

**RIGHT:**

> y'all (contraction of *you all*)
> ain't (a loose contraction of *am not* or *are not*)

## Do not use an apostrophe in most plural words.

**WRONG:**

> Both boy's and girl's are invited to try out for the soccer team.

**RIGHT:**

> Both boys and girls are invited to try out for the soccer team.

**WRONG:**

> Tomato's for sale

**RIGHT:**

> Tomatoes for sale

**WRONG:**

> I grew up in the 1980's.
> (Never use an apostrophe with years.)

**RIGHT:**

> I grew up in the 1980s.

RIGHT:
> There are three 9's on this page.

ALSO RIGHT:
> There are three 9s on this page.
> (With numbers other than years, either way is okay.)

Do use an apostrophe with these plurals:

WORDS USED AS WORDS:
> There are too many *but*'s in that sentence.

ABBREVIATIONS:
> There are three M.D.'s here.

ALPHABET:
> *Mississippi* is spelled with four *s*'s, four *i*'s, and two *p*'s.

# Ellipses

### Use an ellipsis to indicate that some words have been left out of a quotation.

> The governor said, "It is very important for our children
> . . . that the school year be extended . . . and that they go
> to school . . . 360 days a year."

Uh-oh, sounds bad. But you have to be wary with ellipses. What if the newspaper reporter left out some crucial words? What if what the governor really said was this:

> "It is very important for our children to have plenty of play
> time. Some people argue that the school year be
> extended, but I feel that our kids work hard enough and
> that they go to school enough days. Nobody should go to
> school 360 days a year!"

### Use an ellipsis to indicate that something unwritten came earlier.

> " . . . I do," said Cary.

### Use an ellipsis to indicate a sentence trailing off.

Imagine this as the final sentence of a book chapter—it entices you to turn the page to read what happens next:

> Tom and Carlos were camping in the woods, asleep in their tent, when they heard it—the sound . . .

### Use an ellipsis to indicate a long, slow break.

LONG, SLOW BREAK:
> There it was again . . . that soft but eerie sound.

FAST, CRISP BREAK:
> There it was again—that loud, crashing sound.

### Use an ellipsis to indicate slow-downs in thought or conversation.

> They looked sweetly into each other's eyes until the moment was right, then slowly . . . gently . . . a kiss.

# Underlining and italics

### Use italics or underlining for names of books, magazines, newspapers, movies, operas, plays, and other large works.

> *The New York Times*      <u>The New York Times</u>
> *The Addams Family*       <u>The Addams Family</u>
> *Terminator II*           <u>Terminator II</u>

### Use quotation marks (not underlining or italics) for the names of songs, poems, magazine articles, newspaper articles, short stories, chapters of books, and other small works.

SONG:
> "Material Girl"

ARTICLE:
> "Tarheel Women Win Soccer Nationals"

## Use italics or underlining for emphasis.

I really mean it this time: *Don't bite the dog!*
Guess who asked me to the prom—<u>Hartley</u>!
Will I *never* finish this algebra homework?

## Use italics or underlining for foreign words.

<u>RIGHT:</u>
I ordered *coq au vin* for dinner.
<u>ALSO RIGHT:</u>
I ordered <u>coq au vin</u> for dinner.

Some words are so common in English that they aren't considered foreign anymore; for example, patio, kindergarten, quiche, and salsa. But what about piñata and sombrero? Are they foreign or not? It's your call—or consult your dictionary.

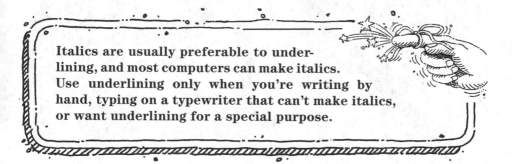

Italics are usually preferable to underlining, and most computers can make italics. Use underlining only when you're writing by hand, typing on a typewriter that can't make italics, or want underlining for a special purpose.

## Use italics or underlining or quotation marks for words used as words.

<u>RIGHT:</u>
*Pneumonia* is a tough word to spell.
<u>ALSO RIGHT:</u>
"Pneumonia" is a tough word to spell.
<u>ALSO RIGHT:</u>
<u>Pneumonia</u> is a tough word to spell.

# Asterisks and bullets

**\* \* \* These are asterisks.**
**• • • These are bullets.**

Asterisks are used to say "look at the bottom of the page for an additional note."\* Asterisks have traditionally been used to highlight or separate information, particularly items in a list. Bullets, however, are now being used more often than asterisks for this purpose because many people use word processors. Notice how bullets are used on page 127.

# Slashes

**Use slashes (or hyphens) with dates.**

> RIGHT:
> 1/1/97
> ALSO RIGHT:
> 1-1-97

**Use a slash with certain pairs of words. Read the slash as *and* or *or*.**

> he/she = he or she
> the soup/salad lunch = the soup and salad lunch
> the March/April issue = the March and April issue

---

\* You get the idea? If you see an asterisk, look at the bottom of the page to find out what the extra information is.

## Use a slash with fractions.

2½    ¹⁶/₁₇

## Use a slash to mean *per.*

60 miles/hour = 60 miles per hour
36 candles/box = 36 candles per box
2 aspirin/day = 2 aspirin per day

# BRAIN TICKLERS
### Set # 9

Find the goofs in these sentences and correct them.

1. I saw two elephant's waltzing in my front yard.

2. The waiter confessed, "You're dinner is ready and there's is ready, but I've forgotten who's dinner is who's. What did you order?"

3. Bill called his sisters names.

4. My dad is great at do-it yourself projects.

5. My uncle is fifty one years old.

6. This dress is to-die-for!

7. We ate three quarter pound lobsters.

8. There was a long line at the restaurant drive through, so I sat in my car with the air-conditioning running and read a news paper.

9. My dad reads "The Wall Street Journal" every day.

10. I liked your article <u>Techniques for Rollerblading on Gravel, Ice, and Snow</u>.

11. I ordered beef. My French friend ordered the same, but he called it boeuf.

12. My mom bought a 10 foot Christmas tree this year.

(Answers are on page 148.)

# Quotation marks

## Use quotation marks to enclose what someone says.

When you use someone's exact words, that is called a direct quotation.

> Mario said, "Get me a Coke," and Elena replied, "Get it yourself."
> My math teacher said, with a frown on her face, "Three plus three does not equal 33, and I suspect you were pulling my leg."

## Do not use quotation marks with indirect quotations.

(See page 86 for more about indirect quotations.)

<u>WRONG:</u>
> Juanita said that she "wants a dwarf killer whale for a pet." (I'm telling you about what Juanita said, but I'm not using her exact words.)

<u>RIGHT:</u>
> Juanita said that she wants a dwarf killer whale for a pet.

<u>ALSO RIGHT:</u>
> Juanita said, "I want a dwarf killer whale for a pet." (Now I'm using Juanita's exact words; this is a direct quotation.)

123

WRONG:
I told Tucker to, "Finish his homework."

RIGHT:
I told Tucker to finish his homework.

## If a quotation is half-direct and half-indirect, don't use quotation marks unless you want to emphasize the quotation.

WRONG:
The newspaper called Josh, "The hero of the game."

RIGHT:
The newspaper called Josh the hero of the game.

ALSO RIGHT:
The newspaper called Josh "the hero of the game."
(Notice there is no comma and *the* is not capitalized.)

ALSO RIGHT [DIRECT QUOTE]:
The newspaper said, "Joshua Zinn was the hero of the game."

WRONG:
Meg referred to her horse as, "A magnificent white steed."

RIGHT:
Meg referred to her horse as a magnificent white steed.

ALSO RIGHT:
Meg referred to her horse as a "magnificent white steed."
(Notice there is no comma and *magnificent* is not capitalized.)

ALSO RIGHT [DIRECT QUOTE]:
Meg said, "My horse is a magnificent white steed."

## Thoughts or questions in someone's mind (in other words, ideas not spoken out loud) do not need quotation marks.

WRONG:
"Will I survive this bungee jump?" Austin wondered.

RIGHT:
Will I survive this bungee jump? Austin wondered.

<u>WRONG:</u>
I've asked myself many times "why eat vegetables?"
<u>RIGHT:</u>
I've asked myself many times, why eat vegetables?

## Use quotation marks to suggest doubt or skepticism.

You call this a "bicycle"? I call it a pile of rusty metal.
The teacher said we did "okay" on the test—whatever that means.

## Use quotation marks, underlining or, best of all, italics for words used as words.

<u>WRONG:</u>
That is a pronoun, I is a pronoun, and you is not a verb.
<u>RIGHT:</u>
"That" is a pronoun, "I" is a pronoun, and "you" is not a verb.
<u>ALSO RIGHT:</u>
*That* is a pronoun, *I* is a pronoun, and *you* is not a verb.
<u>ALSO RIGHT:</u>
<u>That</u> is a pronoun, <u>I</u> is a pronoun, and <u>you</u> is not a verb.

<u>WRONG:</u>
The words a lot are often incorrectly written as alot.
<u>RIGHT:</u>
The words "a lot" are often incorrectly written as "alot."
<u>ALSO RIGHT:</u>
The words *a lot* are often incorrectly written as *alot.*
<u>ALSO RIGHT:</u>
The words <u>a lot</u> are often incorrectly written as <u>alot.</u>

## Use quotation marks for definitions.

One definition of the word *junk* is "a Chinese flat-bottomed ship."

A principle is "a basic truth or a standard of good behavior"; a principal is "one who holds a position of presiding rank, especially the head of a school."

### Use quotation marks for sayings.

My mom loves to use the saying "every dog has its day."

"Don't count your chickens before they hatch" means don't act like something you hope might happen is a sure bet.

### Use quotation marks for labels, markings, signs, etc.

Notice there are no commas before or after these quotation marks.

I'm confused. This stoplight says "stop" and that one says "go."
Stamp the receipts "paid."
Label this container "flour" and that one "sugar."

### Use quotation marks to indicate the clever or silly use of a word.

I love the "flowers" you made out of ribbon and beads.
Ted really "spazzed out" when the teacher asked him to recite the "preambulator" to the Constitution in front of the class.
I am "a-maized" how good this corn tastes!

Don't be too cute. It is a common "goofy goof" to overuse quotation marks in an attempt to be "qute" and clever, drawing attention to certain words in a "ha-ha" or sarcastic ("gimme a break") way. Some students put every single "slangy" word in quotes, and anything that's the least "itsy bitsy" silly gets the "squiggly" little marks, too. Before long their papers look really "b-a-d" when what they intended was to look really "r-a-d." Get the point?

## More on Quotations

Punctuating quotations can be tricky, but if you follow these four simple examples, you'll get it right at least 90 percent of the time.

> Kate said, "Hello."
- Use a comma before the opening quotation mark.
- Use a capital letter to begin the quotation.
- Put the period inside the closing quotation mark.

> Kate said, "Hello," and I asked, "What's up?"
- Use a comma before the opening quotation mark.
- Use a capital letter to begin the quotation.
- Use a comma (not a period) after *hello* because the sentence is not over yet.
- Use a comma before the opening quotation mark of the second quotation.
- Use a capital letter to begin the second quotation because there is a new speaker.

> "I'm hungry," Kate said, "and I'm dying for some chocolate-covered pickles. Do you have any around here?"
- Put the comma inside the quotation mark.
- Use a comma (not a period) after *said* because Kate's first sentence is still going on.
- Do not capitalize *and*—this is not a new sentence. This is still part of Kate's first sentence.
- Do not put a closing quotation mark after *pickles*. Kate is still talking. Don't use the closing quotation mark until she's finished.
- Capitalize *do*—it begins a new sentence.

"Help!" cried Kate. "Without chocolate-covered pickles, I'll surely starve."

- Use a period (not a comma) after *Kate* because Kate is saying two separate sentences.
- Capitalize *without*—it begins a new sentence that Kate is saying.

# Be careful with commas, periods, colons, and semicolons.

## Commas and periods always go *inside* the quotation mark.

WRONG:

Marsha said, "Let's go", and we did.

RIGHT:

Marsha said, "Let's go," and we did.

WRONG:

The title of the song is "River of Dreams".

RIGHT:

The title of the song is "River of Dreams."

## Colons and semicolons always go *outside* the quotation mark.

WRONG:

Catherine said, "I'll clean my room;" now we'll see if she means it.

RIGHT:

Catherine said, "I'll clean my room"; now we'll see if she means it.

WRONG:

Mom uttered the first rule of "parental law:" *just because I said so!*

RIGHT:

Mom uttered the first rule of "parental law": *just because I said so!*

## If you have a quotation within a quotation, use single quotation marks around it.

RIGHT:

    Parker said, "My mom said, 'No way!' "

RIGHT:

    Parker said, "My mom said, 'No way!' so I guess we can't go."

## If only *yes* or *no* is quoted, you don't have to use quotation marks.

RIGHT:

    Jamal said yes.

ALSO RIGHT:

    Jamal said, "Yes."

## If several different speakers are quoted, start a new paragraph for each new speaker.

    All the boys had gathered at Hartley's house. Hartley said, "Does anyone want to play basketball?"

"Sure," replied Syman. "Where's the ball?" He ran toward the basketball court but couldn't find a ball there.

"There's one in the garage," called Hartley. "I'll get it." Hartley went to get the ball while the other kids began to choose teams.

"I want to be on Syman's team!" shouted Ryan.

"Me, too," said Marshall.

"Well, I want to be on Hartley's team," chimed in Wesley.

## Quotations that are questions can be tricky.

Notice when the question mark goes inside the quotation mark and when it goes outside.

If only the quotation is a question:

> **WRONG:**
> Austin asked, "Is that you"?
> **RIGHT:**
> Austin asked, "Is that you?"

If the whole sentence is a question:

> **WRONG:**
> Are you the one who yelled, "Help?"
> **RIGHT:**
> Are you the one who yelled, "Help"?

If both the quotation and the sentence are questions:

> **WRONG:**
> Are you the person who asked, "Why?"?
> **RIGHT:**
> Are you the person who asked, "Why?"

## Quotations that are exclamations can also be tricky.

Notice when the exclamation point goes inside the quotation mark and when it goes outside.

If only the quotation is an exclamation:

> **WRONG:**
> I think he's the one who yelled, "Fire"!

RIGHT:
   I think he's the one who yelled, "Fire!"

If the whole sentence is an exclamation:

WRONG:
   I was furious when he smugly said, "Drop dead!"
RIGHT:
   I was furious when he smugly said, "Drop dead"!

If both the quotation and the sentence are exclamations:

WRONG:
   Oh, no, he's yelling, "Fire!"!
RIGHT:
   Oh, no, he's yelling, "Fire!"

## If a quotation from one person is longer than one paragraph, there is no closing quotation mark until the very end of the quotation.

Each new paragraph begins with an opening quotation mark, but there is no closing quotation mark until the speaker is completely finished.

> Josh said to his math teacher, "I did study for the exam. I really did.
>
> "It's just that I had a slight problem. You see, my math book is printed in Japanese. I know it sounds strange, and it's the only book of its kind, but it's a fact.
>
> "If you don't believe me, I'll be glad to show you.
>
> "So, you see, if you had asked the questions in Japanese, I would have known the answers and probably would have made an A.
>
> "You do believe me, don't you?"

## If you have a long quotation from a book (most writers consider long to be four lines or more), use the block form.

> Rory had sat and watched the patient fingers. There was love in them, and magic. A conjuror's fingers, putting

> back together all the tiny broken pieces, all the cogs and
> wheels. He'd understood what he was watching: his
> dad's fingers trying to put back together the pieces of his
> life, to make it tick again. He'd longed to reach out and
> touch them.
>
> —Nicholas Wilde, *The Eye of the Storm*

The reason for putting long quotations in this format is to help
your reader easily see where the quotation begins and where it
ends. Notice that block quotations

- usually use smaller type than the rest of the text
- use single spacing (or tighter spacing than the rest of
  the text)
- are indented and set off from the rest of the text
- are not enclosed in quotation marks
- include the author's name and book title preceded by
  a dash.

# HIGHLIGHTS: ABBREVIATIONS, NUMBERS, SYMBOLS, AND EMPHASIS

@  #  $  √  18  ≤  %  6.5  ¢  ≠  +

## Abbreviations

**If you're writing a note to yourself or a letter to a friend, use
any symbols and abbreviations you wish.**

However, in formal writing avoid most symbols and
abbreviations.

SAY WHAT?
> On Mon. I traveled E along I-40 past RDU headed for E.
> NC. FYI, I was transporting ½ doz. newborn pug puppies
> (valued at > $100 @) to a kennel, and I wanted to get
> them to their dest. ASAP.

132

**MUCH BETTER:**

On Monday I traveled east along Interstate 40 past Raleigh-Durham airport headed for eastern North Carolina. For your information, I was transporting six newborn pug puppies (valued at over $100 each) to a kennel, and I wanted to get them to their destination as soon as possible.

**WEAK:**

My brother + sister tagged along.

**BETTER:**

My brother and sister tagged along.

**WEAK:**

The swimming pool is 50 ft. long.

**BETTER:**

The swimming pool is 50 feet long.

**WEAK:**

I feel O.K.

**BETTER:**

I feel okay.

<u>WEAK:</u>
We moved to Tenn. from Va.
<u>BETTER:</u>
We moved to Tennessee from Virginia.

<u>WEAK:</u>
I watch too much TV.
<u>BETTER:</u>
I watch too much television.

<u>WEAK:</u>
There are 12 in. in a ft. and 36 in. in a yd.
<u>BETTER:</u>
There are 12 inches in a foot and 36 inches in a yard.

# Titles

## Do use abbreviations with most titles.

They are much easier to read than spelling out the entire title.

<u>RIGHT BUT VERY AWKWARD:</u>
We invited Mister Chan, Mistress Chan, Ms. Sutton, Doctor Stevens, and Bill Stevens, Junior, to our party.
<u>RIGHT AND EASIER TO READ:</u>
We invited Mr. Chan, Mrs. Chan, Ms. Sutton, Dr. Stevens, and Bill Stevens, Jr., to our party.
(Note: *Ms.* exists only as an abbreviation.)

# Numerals

## If you're writing a paper for science class or math class, you would obviously use many more symbols and numerals than you would if you're writing a poem or a short story for language arts class.

<u>RIGHT FOR MATH CLASS:</u>
$2 + 2 = 4$
<u>RIGHT FOR LANGUAGE ARTS CLASS:</u>
Two plus two equals four.

WRONG FOR LANGUAGE ARTS CLASS:
> The 2 are ≠
RIGHT FOR LANGUAGE ARTS CLASS:
> The two are not equal.

## Different writers have different styles when it comes to numbers.

Some write out almost all numbers (even big, hard-to-read numbers such as *one thousand four hundred and twenty*). Most newspapers write out the numbers one through nine and use numerals for 10 and up. One important thing to remember is this: Be consistent!

INCONSISTENT:
> At the zoo we saw thirty-two zebras, 14 elephants, twenty-seven iguanas, and 3 lions.

CONSISTENT:
> At the zoo we saw 32 zebras, 14 elephants, 27 iguanas, and 3 lions.

## Another important thing to remember when writing numbers is to make life easy for your reader.

RIGHT BUT VERY HARD TO READ:
> I'd love to have three thousand six hundred and seventy cats.

RIGHT AND EASY TO READ:
> I'd love to have 3,670 cats.

If you wish, write out numbers above ten as long as they are easy to read.

EASY TO READ:
> I'd love to have two cats—two hundred cats—even two thousand cats.

EASY TO READ:
> Josh says he has dreamed at least a million times about being a tennis pro.

## Don't start a sentence with a numeral.

WRONG:
12,477 fans attended the game.

RIGHT:
Twelve thousand four hundred and seventy-seven fans attended the game.

BETTER:
There were 12,477 fans at the game.

## Here's how to avoid confusion with side-by-side numerals:

CONFUSING:
There were 16 6-foot men playing basketball.

CLEAR:
There were 16 six-foot men playing basketball.

ALSO CLEAR:
There were sixteen six-foot men playing basketball.

# Time

RIGHT BUT HARD TO READ:
Ryan ran the course in three hours, eighteen minutes, and five seconds.
RIGHT AND EASY TO READ:
Ryan ran the course in 3 hours, 18 minutes, and 5 seconds.

RIGHT:
I fell asleep at 10 o'clock in the evening.
EASIER TO READ:
I fell asleep at 10 P.M.
ALSO RIGHT:
I fell asleep at 10:00 P.M.
ALSO RIGHT:
I fell asleep at 10:00 p.m.
(If your computer can do it, put P.M. in small caps. If not, use lowercase.)

# Ages

RIGHT:
I am twelve years old and my mom is thirty-seven years old.
EASIER TO READ:
I am 12 years old and my mom is 37 years old.

# Money

| Right but hard to read | Right and easy to read |
| --- | --- |
| four dollars and fifty cents | $4.50 |
| three point six million dollars | $3.6 million |
| $200,000,000,000 | $200 billion |
| $0.47 | 47 cents (This style is better than writing 47¢.) |

137

# Addresses

## Always use numerals with addresses.

WRONG:
    She lives at three sixty-four Cedar Valley Court.

RIGHT:
    She lives at 364 Cedar Valley Court.

# Dates

WRONG:
    Today is June 19th.
    (We say the *th*, but we don't write it with dates that come
        after the month. Do write the *th* with ordinals, which are
        described next.)

RIGHT:
    Today is June 19.

ALSO RIGHT:
    Today is the 19th.

# Ordinals—1st, 2nd, 3rd, etc. (numbers that indicate position or ranking)

## Write them out if they contain just one word.

INFORMAL:
    Wesley was the 1st person ever to water ski on his head.

BETTER:
    Wesley was the first person ever to water ski on his head.

<u>INFORMAL:</u>
Marshall ranks 10th in his school and 20th in the state.
<u>BETTER:</u>
Marshall ranks tenth in his school and twentieth in
the state.

## Use numerals if an ordinal contains more than one word.

<u>RIGHT BUT HARD TO READ:</u>
Joe is ranked thirty-second in the state, and Sue is ranked
one hundred twenty-sixth.
<u>EASIER TO READ:</u>
Joe is ranked 32nd in the state, and Sue is ranked 126th.

# Chapters and page numbers

## Always use numerals with page numbers and usually with chapters.

<u>RIGHT:</u>
Read chapter 6, pages 101-109.
<u>ALSO RIGHT:</u>
Read chapter six, pages 101-109.

# Measurements, weights, and temperatures

<u>RIGHT:</u>
Her baby is a beautiful seven-pound, ten-ounce boy.
<u>EASIER TO READ:</u>
Her baby is a beautiful 7-pound, 10-ounce boy.

<u>RIGHT:</u>
It's only sixteen degrees outside!
<u>EASIER TO READ:</u>
It's only 16 degrees outside!

<u>RIGHT:</u>
The size of the room is twenty feet by twenty feet.
<u>EASIER TO READ:</u>
The size of the room is 20 feet by 20 feet.

> Should 100 be *a hundred* or should it be
> *100*? It all depends. Consider the context: is
> this a math paper or a poem? Is it a physics final
> exam or a love letter? Usually go with whatever is
> quicker for the eye to grab and, therefore, easier for
> your reader to read.

## CREATING EMPHASIS

How can you draw attention to certain words or phrases in your writing? Notice how "Creating Emphasis" is written—exciting, isn't it? Well, you can't use fancy fonts all the time. Here are some ways you can do it with punctuation.

Imagine that your cousin Jeff has been presumed dead for three years. One night there's a knock at the door. You open the door and . . .

> When I opened the door, I couldn't believe my eyes. It
> was Jeff.
>> I couldn't believe my eyes: it was Jeff.
>> I couldn't believe my eyes: it was Jeff!
>> I couldn't believe my eyes—it was Jeff!
>> I couldn't believe my eyes. *It was Jeff!*
>> I couldn't believe my eyes . . . Jeff!
>> I couldn't believe my eyes—JEFF!
>> I couldn't believe my eyes—<u>JEFF</u>!

Be careful not to overdo emphasis. Too little makes your writing dull, but too much makes your writing look silly.

Speaking of silly, check this out:

> Holy cow! I could *hardly* believe how incredibly <u>lucky</u> I
> was!! I played HARD this season, but I really didn't ex-
> pect to win (yes, win!!) the coveted *t-r-o-p-h-y*. What a

surprise! I was in total awe . . . and I do mean *total*, as in—wow!—**mega-total**.

A bit too much emphasis, don't you think?

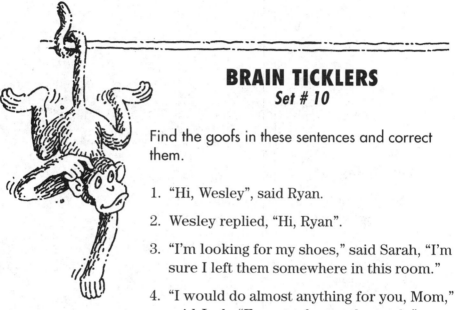

## BRAIN TICKLERS
### Set # 10

Find the goofs in these sentences and correct them.

1. "Hi, Wesley", said Ryan.

2. Wesley replied, "Hi, Ryan".

3. "I'm looking for my shoes," said Sarah, "I'm sure I left them somewhere in this room."

4. "I would do almost anything for you, Mom," said Josh. "Except take out the trash."

5. The words <u>school's</u> <u>out</u> are music to my ears.

6. What does the saying a penny saved is a penny earned mean?

7. I found a box in the attic labeled, "Baseball cards," and another labeled, "Old photos."

8. "How are you?", I asked Erica.

9. I read the poem "Ode to a Toad;" I liked it a lot.

10. Meg asked whether she "could sleep over at Eliza's house."

11. I was sad when she yelled, "I hate you"!

12. Did you ask, "Why me"?

13. Dad gave me "big bucks" (two "whole" dollars) to spend at the "card show."

14. Bill said, "Becca said, yes, I'll help you, but she didn't."

15. "When will it be time for dinner?" I wonder.

16. My birthday is Aug. 23rd.

17. Wow! SUPER DOOPER g!o!l!l!y The chapter is over!!

(Answers are on page 150.)

# BRAIN TICKLERS— THE ANSWERS

## Set # 6, page 92

1. At the fair, I ate cotton candy, a caramel apple and, a foot-long hot dog.

   What's the comma doing after *and*? Put a comma before *and*, not after. At the fair, I ate cotton candy, a caramel apple, and a foot-long hot dog.

2. I pigged out on food at the fair, and got a stomachache as a result.

   These are not two separate sentences joined by a conjunction. (*Got a stomachache as a result* is not a sentence.) Both of these are correct:
   • I pigged out on food at the fair and got a stomachache as a result.
   • I pigged out on food at the fair, and I got a stomachache as a result.

3. Dad was tired but, he kept driving until we finally arrived at the beach.

   These are two separate sentences joined by a conjunction, but the comma is in the wrong place. It always goes before the conjunction, never after it. Dad was tired, but he kept driving until we finally arrived at the beach.

4. Whatever you do do it well.

   *Whatever you do* is an introductory clause. It's quite short, so a comma is not absolutely necessary, but this sentence is confusing without the comma. This is much clearer: Whatever you do, do it well.

5. I live in a charming, old, nineteenth-century, house.

   What's the comma doing before *house*? Delete it. I live in a charming, old, nineteenth-century house.

6. Today is Wednesday December 25, 1996.

   There's a comma missing. Put one after *Wednesday*.

7. People from Raleigh, North Carolina often vacation at Myrtle Beach, South Carolina.

   There's a comma missing. Put one after *North Carolina*.

8. I admit that yes I did put that turtle in the toilet.

   Two commas are missing. I admit that, yes, I did put that turtle in the toilet.

9. The tall guy on the basketball team Legs Long is my neighbor.

   *Legs Long* is an appositive—it tells more about *the tall guy on the team*. It needs commas. The tall guy on the basketball team, Legs Long, is my neighbor.

10. The new kid on the tennis team whom I beat last week won the tournament.

    This is correct if there are several new kids on the tennis team and you're specifically talking about the one you beat last week. In that case, the clause *whom I beat last week* is necessary and does not need commas. If, on the other hand, there is only one new kid on the team, then the clause *whom I beat last week* is not necessary (it's a by-the-way clause) and commas are needed: The new kid on the tennis team, whom I beat last week, won the tournament.

11. Everyone, who hasn't finished the test, must stay after school to finish it.

    The commas around the clause *who hasn't finished the test* indicate that this is a by-the-way clause—in other words, you can delete it and the sentence will still make sense. Let's try it: *Everyone must stay after school to finish it.* Oops, that's not what you meant to say, is it? This is correct: Everyone who hasn't finished the test must stay after school to finish it.

12. At sunset beach walks are beautiful.

    There's nothing incorrect here, but the sentence is a little confusing. A comma would help. At sunset, beach walks are beautiful.

13. I know I said I'd be there at 9:00, but hey I didn't count on twelve inches of snow.

    Put commas before and after interjections. I know I said I'd be there at 9:00, but, hey, I didn't count on twelve inches of snow.

14. I called you Becca just to say hello.

    Did you call Becca to say hello or did you call somebody "Becca" in order to say hello? I think this is what you mean: I called you, Becca, just to say hello.

15. Allison bought a lacy, bright, red dress.

    Where would you put *and*'s? "Bright red" sounds better than "bright and red," so let's leave out that comma. "Lacy and bright red" sounds fine, so let's leave that one in. Allison bought a lacy, bright red dress.

16. Dr Austin Stevens and Gov Hartley Hsu were at the meeting.

    Some abbreviations need periods; Dr. and Gov. definitely do. Dr. Austin Stevens and Gov. Hartley Hsu were at the meeting.

17. Did the package arrive c.o.d?

    Notice the final period. Did the package arrive c.o.d.?

18. I wonder whether it's going to rain?

    This is an indirect question; change the question mark to a period. I wonder whether it's going to rain.

19. Why did you bring your math teacher a bouquet of flowers instead of bringing her your overdue homework assignment, I wondered?

    The question mark is in the wrong place. Why did you bring your math teacher a bouquet of flowers instead of bringing her your overdue homework assignment? I wondered.

20. The huge dinosaurs, creatures of the distant past, pictured on the pages of history books roaming vast plains a million years ago, with their gazing eyes and huge bodies, lumbering along with no concern for what lay in their paths, creating terror wherever they roamed.

    That's a fine bunch of words, but it's not a sentence. This is actually one very very long subject, but we don't know what the dinosaurs did. A simple word change here or there would make all the difference. The huge dinosaurs, creatures of the distant past pictured on the pages of history books, roamed vast plains a million years ago; with their gazing eyes and huge bodies, they lumbered along with no concern for what lay in their paths, creating terror wherever they roamed.

# Set # 7, page 100

1. I want to see the new ninja movie, I want to see the new Addams Family movie, too.

    Two separate sentences are joined by a comma. That won't do! Either join them with a semicolon or separate them with a period. Both of these are correct:
    • I want to see the new ninja movie; I want to see the new Addams Family movie, too.
    • I want to see the new ninja movie. I want to see the new Addams Family movie, too.

2. When you go to the store, please pick up: apples, bread, and juice.

   Don't use a colon if the list comes immediately after the verb, as it does here. (The verb is *pick up*.) Both of these are correct:
   - When you go to the store, please pick up apples, bread, and juice.
   - When you go the store, please pick up the following: apples, bread, and juice.

3. Mom said that only one thing will earn me an increase in allowance: A consistently clean room.

   Capitalize the first word after a colon only if it begins a complete sentence. *A consistently clean room* is not a complete sentence. Mom said that only one thing will earn me an increase in allowance: a consistently clean room.

4. I love the colors green, blue, and red, the names Vanessa, Charlotte, and Cassandra, the states Iowa, Idaho, and Illinois, but not the foods anchovies, olives, and eggplant.

   Very confusing! This sentence needs to be given a healthy dose of semicolons. I love the colors green, blue, and red; the names Vanessa, Charlotte, and Cassandra; the states Iowa, Idaho, and Illinois; but not the foods anchovies, olives, and eggplant.

5. I was on the swim team last year, we had a winning season.

   A comma is not strong enough to separate two complete sentences. You have three options for cleaning up this sentence:
   - I was on the swim team last year; we had a winning season.
   - I was on the swim team last year, and we had a winning season.
   - I was on the swim team last year. We had a winning season.

6. I like chocolate cake; my dad cooks great spaghetti.

   These two sentences are not closely related, so the semicolon is wrong. Here are two possible ways to clean it up:

- I like chocolate cake. My dad cooks great spaghetti.
- Two of my favorite foods are chocolate cake and my dad's great spaghetti. (Notice that this sentence creates a link between chocolate cake and spaghetti, so it now makes sense to put them in the same sentence.)

7. This is the weather report for tomorrow, heavy rain, gusty winds, and a chance of flooding.

   A comma is not strong enough here. This is the weather report for tomorrow: heavy rain, gusty winds, and a chance of flooding.

8. I hoped it would snow, finally, it did.

   A comma is not strong enough here. Both of these are correct:
   - I hoped it would snow. Finally, it did.
   - I hoped it would snow; finally, it did.

# Set # 8, page 109

1. Don't even think of trying to buy beer (It's against the law.) before you're 21 years old.

   We have a complete sentence embedded in another sentence. Even though it seems odd, don't use a capital letter to begin it and don't use a period at the end. Don't even think of trying to buy beer (it's against the law) before you're 21 years old.

2. It is dangerous (potentially deadly)! to drink and drive.

   The exclamation mark is in the wrong place. It is dangerous (potentially deadly!) to drink and drive.

3. There is only one thing I need to be happy (or I should say *really* happy:) chocolate.

   The colon is in the wrong place. There is only one thing I need to be happy (or I should say *really* happy): chocolate.

4. I am excited (really excited!) about the party.

This is okay, but parentheses "hide" information. With this much emphasis, dashes might be better. I am excited—really excited!—about the party.

5. I want three things for Christmas, video games, rollerblades, and baseball cards.

The comma after *Christmas* won't do. It's much too weak for the job. Here are two ways to clean up this sentence:
- I want three things for Christmas—video games, roller-blades, and baseball cards.
- I want three things for Christmas: video games, roller-blades, and baseball cards.

## Set # 9, page 122

1. I saw two elephant's waltzing in my front yard.

*Elephants* should be plural, not possessive. Delete the apostrophe. I saw two elephants waltzing in my front yard.

2. The waiter confessed, "You're dinner is ready and there's is ready, but I've forgotten who's dinner is who's. What did you order?"

Yikes! What a mess. Did you catch all these apostrophe goofs? <u>Your</u> dinner is ready and <u>theirs</u> is ready, but I've forgotten <u>whose</u> dinner is <u>whose</u>.

3. Bill called his sisters names.

Very tricky. The apostrophe [*sisters* or *sister's* or *sisters'*] makes all the difference. This sentence is correct if you mean that Bill called his sisters (more than one) bad names. But maybe you mean one of these:
- Bill called [yelled out] his [one] <u>sister's</u> [Katie's] names [Katie, Katherine, Kat, little sis].
- Bill called [yelled out] his <u>sisters'</u> [perhaps Katie's and Becca's] names.

4. My dad is great at do-it yourself projects.

   *Do-it-yourself* is a compound adjective describing *projects*. It is meant to be read as one word, so it needs hyphens. It is a common mistake to stop short and hyphenate only part of a phrase. My dad is great at <u>do-it-yourself</u> projects.

5. My uncle is fifty one years old.

   A hyphen is needed. My uncle is <u>fifty-one</u> years old.

6. This dress is to-die-for!

   If a compound adjective comes before the noun, use hyphens. (For example: This is a <u>to-die-for</u> dress!) If a compound adjective comes after the noun, don't use hyphens. This is correct: This dress is <u>to die for</u>!

7. We ate three quarter pound lobsters.

   Tricky! Do you mean you ate lobsters that weighed three-quarters of a pound? Or that you ate 3 quarter-pound lobsters? Both of these are correct:
   • We ate three quarter-pound lobsters.
   • We ate three-quarter-pound lobsters.

8. There was a long line at the restaurant drive through, so I sat in my car with the air-conditioning running and read a news paper.

   Some compound nouns are two words, some are one word, and some are hyphenated. Check your dictionary! In this case, this is right: There was a long line at the restaurant <u>drive-through</u>, so I sat in my car with the <u>air conditioning</u> running and read a <u>newspaper</u>.

9. My dad reads "The Wall Street Journal" every day.

   Names of newspapers should be underlined or put in italics. Both of these are correct:
   • My dad reads *The Wall Street Journal* every day.
   • My dad reads <u>The Wall Street Journal</u> every day.

10. I liked your article <u>Techniques for Rollerblading on Gravel, Ice, and Snow</u>.

    Large works such as books are underlined or written in italics; small works are put in quotation marks. An article is considered a small work. I liked your article "Techniques for Rollerblading on Gravel, Ice, and Snow."

11. I ordered beef. My French friend ordered the same, but he called it boeuf.

    Use underlining or italics for foreign words. Both of these are correct:
    • My French friend ordered the same, but he called it *boeuf*.
    • My French friend ordered the same, but he called it <u>boeuf</u>.

12. My mom bought a 10 foot Christmas tree this year.

    A hyphen is needed. My mom bought a 10-foot Christmas tree this year.

## Set # 10, page 141

1. "Hi, Wesley", said Ryan.

   Always put commas *inside* the quotation mark. "Hi, Wesley," said Ryan.

2. Wesley replied, "Hi, Ryan".

   Always put periods *inside* the quotation mark. Wesley replied, "Hi, Ryan."

3. "I'm looking for my shoes," said Sarah, "I'm sure I left them somewhere in this room."

   These are two separate sentences spoken by Sarah. The two sentences should be separated by a period. "I'm looking for my shoes," said Sarah. "I'm sure I left them somewhere in this room."

4. "I would do almost anything for you, Mom," said Josh. "Except take out the trash."

Josh is saying only one sentence, so *except* should not be capitalized (it doesn't begin a new sentence) and there should not be a period after *Josh* (the sentence isn't over). "I would do almost anything for you, Mom," said Josh, "except take out the trash."

5. The words <u>school's</u> <u>out</u> are music to my ears.

Underlining is not good here. Use quotations.
The words "school's out" are music to my ears.

6. What does the saying a penny saved is a penny earned mean?

Confusing! Use quotation marks for expressions.
What does the saying "a penny saved is a penny earned" mean?

7. I found a box in the attic labeled, "Baseball cards," and another labeled, "Old photos."

These are not quotations—they are labels. With labels, titles, signs, or markings, punctuate this way: I found a box in the attic labeled "baseball cards" and another labeled "old photos."

8. "How are you?", I asked Erica.

What's the comma doing in this sentence? The question mark takes the place of the comma. "How are you?" I asked Erica.

9. I read the poem "Ode to a Toad;" I liked it a lot.

Semicolons go *outside* quotation marks. I read the poem "Ode to a Toad"; I liked it a lot.

10. Meg asked whether she "could sleep over at Eliza's house."

This is an indirect quotation. I'm telling you what Meg said but I'm not quoting her exact words. Therefore, quotation marks are not used. Meg asked whether she could sleep over at Eliza's house.

11. I was sad when she yelled, "I hate you"!

    The quotation is an exclamation, but the whole sentence is not. I was sad when she yelled, "I hate you!"

12. Did you ask, "Why me"?

    The question mark is in the wrong place. Both the quotation and the whole sentence are questions. Did you ask, "Why me?"

13. Dad gave me "big bucks" (two "whole" dollars) to spend at the "card show."

    "Big bucks" indicates you're joking; that one is okay. The other two ("whole" and "card show") are unnecessary and silly. This is better: Dad gave me "big bucks" (two whole dollars) to spend at the card show.

14. Bill said, "Becca said, yes, I'll help you, but she didn't."

    This is a quotation within a quotation. Bill said, "Becca said, 'Yes, I'll help you,' but she didn't."

15. "When will it be time for dinner?" I wonder.

    Thoughts and questions in the mind don't take quotation marks. When will it be time for dinner? I wonder.

16. My birthday is Aug. 23rd.

    Don't abbreviate *August* and don't use the *-rd* when the date comes right after the month. Both of these are correct:
    • My birthday is August 23.
    • My birthday is the 23rd of August.

17. Wow! SUPER DOOPER g!o!l!l!y!! The chapter is over!!

    Much too much emphasis—and silly emphasis to boot. How about this: Wow! The chapter is over.

# Agreement

I think we can agree that agreement is a good thing. Right? Kids agreeing with their parents, boys agreeing with girls, teachers agreeing with students, verbs agreeing with subjects, pronouns agreeing with antecedents—these are good things. I'm sure you don't have a bit of trouble telling whether your parents agree with you about raising your allowance, but can you tell when a verb agrees with its subject? This is tricky territory, so read carefully. When you can consistently tell the difference between grammatical agreement and disagreement, your writing will soar to new heights.

# AGREEMENT BETWEEN SUBJECT AND VERB

## Make sure the verb agrees with the subject.

A singular subject needs a singular verb, and a plural subject needs a plural verb. (Reminder: The verb is the action word in the sentence. The subject is who or what does the action. See page 23 for more about verbs; see page 71 for more about subjects.)

> The girl [singular subject] reads [singular verb] mystery stories.
> The girls [plural subject] read [plural verb] mystery stories.
>
> Meg [singular subject] is [singular verb] asleep.
> Meg and her friends [plural subject] are [plural verb] asleep.

No big deal? Usually not, but just in case you find yourself confused, here are a few reminders.

## Don't be confused by plural words that come after the verb.

> WRONG:
> My biggest problem are the many incomplete homework assignments I need to finish.
> RIGHT:
> My biggest problem [singular subject] is [singular verb] the many incomplete homework assignments I need to finish.

## Don't be confused by plural words that come between a singular subject and the verb.

**WRONG:**
The topic of these four books are horses.

**RIGHT:**
The topic [singular subject] of these four books is [singular verb] horses.

**WRONG:**
Each of the bikes have new tires.

**RIGHT:**
Each [singular subject] of the bikes has [singular verb] new tires.

**WRONG:**
Every one of the members of both basketball teams are here.

**RIGHT:**
Every one [singular subject] of the members of both basket-ball teams is [singular verb] here.

## Don't be confused by subjects that come at the end of the sentence.

**WRONG:**
Standing at the back of the room was my parents.
(Turn the sentence around and it will be clearer: My par-ents were standing at the back of the room.)

**RIGHT:**
Standing at the back of the room were [plural verb] my parents [plural subject].

**WRONG:**
At the end of most of our team's games come victory's sweetness.
(Turn the sentence around: Victory's sweetness comes at the end of most of our team's games.)

**RIGHT:**
At the end of most of our team's games comes [singular verb] victory's sweetness [singular subject].

# Don't be confused by phrases such as *along with, together with, accompanied by, as well as, including,* and *in addition to.*

<u>WRONG:</u>

Tenita, as well as Mike, play basketball well.

<u>RIGHT:</u>

Tenita [singular subject], as well as Mike, plays [singular verb] basketball well.

<u>WRONG:</u>

Broccoli, in addition to squash and all other vegetables, are good for you.

<u>RIGHT:</u>

Broccoli [singular subject], in addition to squash and all other vegetables, is [singular verb] good for you.

# Don't be confused by a *not* phrase.

<u>WRONG:</u>

I, not you, are late.

<u>RIGHT:</u>

I [singular subject], not you, am [singular verb] late.

# Don't be confused by collective nouns.

A collective noun names a group of people or things. Here are some examples: family, orchestra, group, committee, jury, crowd, herd, audience, pair, and squad. Are these nouns singular or plural? They can be either, and you as the writer must decide. Ask yourself whether you're talking about the group as a whole or the individuals within the group.

SINGULAR:
> The football team [the team as a whole] wants to win.

PLURAL:
> The football team [each individual player] put on their uniforms.

SINGULAR:
> The newly married couple [as a whole] is happy.

PLURAL:
> A couple of people were late for the wedding.

WRONG:
> The jury are returning with their decision. (Juries always operate as a whole when they make decisions.)

RIGHT:
> The jury is returning with its decision.

## Don't be confused by nouns of amount.

These are like collective nouns. Ask yourself whether you're talking about the amount as a whole or individual units.

SINGULAR:
> Five hundred dollars is a lot of money.

PLURAL:
> We have a problem: five hundred-dollar bills are missing.

SINGULAR:
> Thirteen pounds is a lot for a newborn baby to weigh.

PLURAL:
> I feel fat. Thirteen of these extra pounds need to come off.

SINGULAR:
> Three hours is a long time to wait.

PLURAL:
> Three separate hours on three separate days were needed to finish the exam.

The word *number* is weird. If you say "the number," it's singular. If you say "a number of," it's plural.

SINGULAR:
The number of kids here is surprisingly large.
PLURAL:
A number of kids are here.

## Don't be confused by indefinite pronouns.

*I* and *you* refer to specific people. Some other pronouns point to non-specific people—for example, *someone, anyone, nobody,* and *anybody.* These are called indefinite pronouns.

Pronouns beginning with *any* (anyone, anybody, etc.), *no* (no one, nobody, nothing), *every* (everyone, everything, etc.), and *some* (something, someone, etc.) are always singular and take a singular verb.

> Everybody is [singular] coming.
> Nothing is [singular] happening.

Here are some other singular pronouns—*each, another, either, neither, little, much.* Each of these pronouns needs a singular verb.

> Little is [singular] happening because neither of my friends is [singular] here.
> The roller coaster ride is finished; another costs [singular] $5.00.

159

Some indefinite pronouns are always plural—*both, several, few, many, most, others*. Each of these pronouns needs a plural verb.

> The Martin girls are twins. Both are [plural] here.
> I like possums. Several are [plural] living in the woods behind my house.

Some indefinite pronouns can be either singular or plural—*any, more, some, enough, all, most, who, half, none*. The rest of the sentence tells you whether to use a singular verb or a plural verb.

> All the cake is gone. (*cake* is singular—use a singular verb)
> All the boys are gone. (*boys* is plural—use a plural verb)
>
> Most of the pie was eaten. (*pie* is singular—use a singular verb)
> Most of the hot dogs were eaten. (*hot dogs* is plural—use a plural verb)
>
> None of the snow has melted. (*snow* is singular—use a singular verb)
> None of the apples are ripe. (*apples* is plural—use a plural verb)
>
> The boy who is late for class sits near me. (*boy* is singular—use singular verbs)
> The boys who are late for class sit near me. (*boys* is plural—use plural verbs)

## Don't be confused by *either/or* and *neither/nor*.

> Either Ryan or Wesley is [singular] here.
>    (Both parts are singular, so use a singular verb.)
> Neither the boys nor the girls are [plural] here.
>    (Both parts are plural, so use a plural verb.)
> Neither the boys nor their mother is [singular] here.
>    (One part is plural and one part is singular. The singular part comes right before the verb, so use a singular verb.)
> Neither the mother nor her sons are [plural] here.
>    (One part is plural and one part is singular. The plural part comes right before the verb, so use a plural verb.)

<u>WRONG:</u>
Either Kristen or Katie are dancing the part of Aurora in the ballet.

<u>RIGHT:</u>
Either Kristen or Katie is dancing the part of Aurora in the ballet.

## Don't be confused by noun phrases referring to a single unit.

Sometimes a noun phrase sounds plural but describes something we think of as a single unit. These noun phrases take a singular verb.

Spaghetti and meatballs is [singular] my favorite dinner.
Ice cream and cake is [singular] my favorite dessert.
Peanut butter and jelly is [singular] my favorite sandwich.

<u>BUT:</u>
Broccoli and spinach are [plural] my favorite vegetables.
(We don't think of broccoli and spinach as parts of a single unit.)

## Don't be confused by nouns that look plural but are actually singular.

The news [singular] is bad.
Measles [singular] is contagious.

Mumps [singular] is contagious, too.
Mathematics [singular] is my easiest class.

## Don't be confused by some -ics nouns that can be either singular or plural.

SINGULAR:
Politics is an interesting career.
PLURAL:
The politics in the presidential campaign were mighty dirty.

SINGULAR:
Statistics is my most interesting class.
PLURAL:
The statistics of the game are not good for our team.

Other -ics nouns that work this way: athletics, acoustics

## Don't be confused by the plural forms of foreign words.

WRONG:
The data shows that boys watch more sports on TV than girls watch.
RIGHT:
The data [plural of datum] show [plural verb] that boys watch more sports on TV than girls watch.

(See page 11 for more about the plural forms of foreign words.)

## Don't be confused by mathematical phrases.

WRONG:
One and one are two.
(If you were talking about one dog and one cat, you would use are. In this case, "one and one" is an idea or concept, not two separate numbers standing stand by side.)
RIGHT:
One and one is two.

**WRONG:**

Five times six are thirty.

("Five times six" is an idea. Have you ever seen a five go up and times a six?)

**RIGHT:**

Five times six is thirty.

# BRAIN TICKLERS
## Set # 11

Find the goofs in these sentences and correct them.

1. The family live on Elm Street.

2. The orchestra tunes its instruments.

3. My pair of scissors are lost.

4. Eight pounds of grapes are a lot of grapes.

5. One of the Martin twins are absent today.

6. The company Video Games Galore are holding their annual picnic on Thursday.

7. Do either of the Joneses live here?

8. Macaroni and cheese are Emily's favorite do-it-yourself dinner.

9. The only problem we 500 campers have are the hundreds of wasps swarming around our ten campsites.

10. Standing there looking happy was Wesley and Austin.

11. Only one out of four kids in America eat a healthy diet.

12. I can't find my catcher's glove; I hope either David or the Joneses has it.

13. Tennis, as well as cycling and swimming, are great aerobic sports.

14. Kate, not I, want to be finished with these exercises.

(Answers are on page 168.)

# AGREEMENT BETWEEN PRONOUNS AND ANTECEDENTS

(Reminder: An antecedent is the noun that a pronoun stands for. See page 16 for more about pronouns and antecedents.)

## A pronoun must agree with its antecedent in gender (male or female).

Not many people make this goof:

**WRONG:**
Each of the girls puts his stuff into the car.
**RIGHT:**
Each of the girls puts her stuff into the car.

## A pronoun must agree with its antecedent in person.

First person (the person talking): I, we
Second person (the person I'm talking to): you
Third person (the person I'm talking about): she, he, it, they

**WRONG:**
If students refuse to learn the rules of proper writing, you can forget a good grade in language arts.
(*You* is a pronoun; *students* is the noun it stands for. *Students* is someone the writer is talking about, so it's third person; *you* is second person.)
**RIGHT:**
If students [third person] refuse to learn the rules of proper writing, they [third person] can forget a good grade in language arts.

## A pronoun must agree with its antecedent in number (singular or plural).

<u>WRONG:</u>
> Each girl wants to look beautiful on their prom night.
> (*Girl* is singular; *their* is plural.)

<u>RIGHT:</u>
> Each girl wants to look beautiful on her prom night.

<u>WRONG:</u>
> If people want to stay healthy, you must eat well and watch your waistline.
> (*People* is third person; *you* and *your* are second person.)

<u>STILL WRONG:</u>
> If people want to stay healthy, they must eat well and watch their waistline.
> (*Waistline* is singular. Do they really have just one waistline?)

<u>RIGHT:</u>
> If people want to stay healthy, they must eat well and watch their waistlines.

# A boy/girl thing

<u>OFTEN USED BUT WRONG:</u>
> If anybody is late, they'll get in trouble.
> (*Anybody* is singular; *they* is plural.)

<u>RISKY:</u>
> If anybody is late, he'll get in trouble.
> (Many people feel it's sexist always to use *he*.)

<u>BETTER:</u>
> If anybody is late, he or she will get in trouble.
> (This is grammatically correct but awkward.)

<u>EVEN BETTER:</u>
> Anyone who is late will get in trouble.

Until recently, writers always used *he* to mean "an unnamed, unspecified person." Is it fair to always use *he*? What about us girls?

**PROBLEM:**

Everyone wants to eat their dessert before dinner.

(This is becoming acceptable in everyday speech and writing, but it is technically wrong. I wouldn't recommend using it in formal writing.)

**SOLUTION #1:**

Everyone wants to eat her dessert before dinner.

(Throughout a paper, you can alternate, sometimes using *he* and sometimes using *she*. You'll often see this in books, but it can be confusing to your reader.)

**SOLUTION #2:**

Everyone wants to eat his/her dessert before dinner.

(Repeatedly using *his/her, he/she,* or *s/he* gets tedious for the reader.)

**SOLUTION #3:**

All the kids want to eat their dessert before dinner.

(Make the subject plural by rewriting the sentence so you can correctly use the nonsexist *they*.)

**SOLUTION #4 (Is this crazy or what?):**

Why don't you come up with a brand new pronoun (not *he,* not *she,* how about *sha* or *yoblrig* or *blagernik*?) and convince everyone who speaks English to use it when he/she means *he/she* or *his/her.* Then we wouldn't have this boy/girl problem!

# Watching out for *there's* and *there is*

Does this sound good to you?

There's only three things I need in life: chocolate, chocolate, and chocolate.

Yes, it sounds great—the chocolate, that is. The sentence, however, is wrong.

**RIGHT:**

There are only three things I need in life: chocolate, chocolate, and chocolate.

*There's* is a contraction: there is = there's. This word slips into speech and writing like a sneaky fox. Be alert. At least make it agree; at best, ax it.

WRONG:
   There's a lot of things we need to discuss before I give you
   a raise in your allowance.

RIGHT:
   There are a lot of things we need to discuss before I give
   you a raise in your allowance.

BETTER:
   We need to discuss a lot of things before I give you a raise
   in your allowance.

WRONG:
   Where's all those monsters you said live under your bed?

RIGHT:
   Where are all those monsters you said live under your
   bed?

# BRAIN TICKLERS
### Set # 12

Find the goofs in these sentences and correct
them.

1. Almost everyone likes watching fireworks
   on the Fourth of July, don't they?

2. Everybody loves their mother.

3. Wait a minute, Miranda. It's very cold
   outside. Here's your coat and hat.

4. I see Robin and Kacey, but where's the other kids?

5. Every player on the team played their best.

6. Either Kate or Meg might lend me their bike.

7. During the scary part of the movie, we could all feel a lot of
   fear rushing through our body.

8. There's a lot of good reasons to learn the rules of proper writing.

9. I don't like these kind of movies.

10. All the girls wore a dress to the dance.

(Answers are on page 170.)

# BRAIN TICKLERS— THE ANSWERS

## Set # 11, page 163

1. The family live on Elm Street.

   *Family* is a collective noun and can be singular or plural, but in this case we are clearly talking about the family as a whole. It should be this: The family <u>lives</u> on Elm Street.

2. The orchestra tunes its instruments.

   *Orchestra* is a collective noun and can be singular or plural, but in this case we are clearly talking about each individual musician tuning his or her instrument.

   **RIGHT:**
   The orchestra tune their instruments.
   **BETTER:**
   The musicians in the orchestra tune their instruments.

3. My pair of scissors are lost.

   *Scissors* is always plural, so it would seem that *are* is the correct verb. However, in this sentence the subject is not *scissors*—it's *pair*. The word *pair*, even though it means two of something, is singular. (Yes, English is sometimes a very wacky language.) Both of these are correct:
   • My pair of scissors <u>is</u> lost.
   • My scissors <u>are</u> lost.

4. Eight pounds of grapes are a lot of grapes.

   In this case, *eight pounds* is a single unit. Eight pounds of grapes <u>is</u> a lot of grapes.

5. One of the Martin twins are absent today.

   The subject of this sentence is *one*, not *twins*. *One* is always singular. One of the Martin twins <u>is</u> absent today.

6. The company Video Games Galore are holding their annual picnic on Thursday.

   Video Games Galore is the name of a company, so it is singular. The company Video Games Galore <u>is</u> holding <u>its</u> annual picnic on Thursday.

7. Do either of the Joneses live here?

   This sounds okay, doesn't it? The problem is that *Joneses* is not the subject of the sentence. *Either* is the subject, and it's singular. It should be this: <u>Does</u> either of the Joneses live here?

8. Macaroni and cheese are Emily's favorite do-it-yourself dinner.

   We think of macaroni and cheese as a single unit, so it needs a singular verb. Macaroni and cheese <u>is</u> Emily's favorite do-it-yourself dinner.

9. The only problem we 500 campers have are the hundreds of wasps swarming around our 10 campsites.

   The subject of this sentence is *problem*, and it is singular. The verb agrees with the subject no matter how many other plural words are floating around. The only problem we 500 campers have <u>is</u> the hundreds of wasps swarming around our 10 campsites.

10. Standing there looking happy was Wesley and Austin.

    Turn it around: *Wesley and Austin was standing there.* That's no good. Standing there looking happy <u>were</u> Wesley and Austin.

11. Only one out of four kids in America eat a healthy diet.

This is a sad statement about our times, but that's not our concern here. What we need to know is, what's the subject? *One* is the subject and it's singular. Only one out of four kids in America <u>eats</u> a healthy diet.

12. I can't find my catcher's glove; I hope either David or the Joneses has it.

*The Joneses* comes closer to the verb. It's plural, so a plural verb is needed. I can't find my catcher's glove; I hope either David or the Joneses <u>have</u> it.

13. Tennis, as well as cycling and swimming, are great aerobic sports.

The subject of the sentence is *tennis*, and it is singular. Don't be confused by *as well as* and similar phrases. Tennis, as well as cycling and swimming, <u>is</u> a great aerobic sport.

14. Kate, not I, want to be finished with these exercises.

*Kate* is the singular subject of the sentence. Kate, not I, <u>wants</u> to be finished with these exercises.

## Set # 12, page 167

1. Almost everyone likes watching fireworks on the Fourth of July, don't they?

This is how we speak, but it's not how we write. *Everyone* is singular, *they* is plural. Both of these are correct:
- Almost everyone likes watching fireworks on the Fourth of July, right?
- Almost all people like watching fireworks on the Fourth of July, don't they?

2. Everybody loves their mother.

*Everybody* is singular, *their* is plural, *mother* is singular. Here are two possible solutions:
- Everybody loves his or her mother.
- People love their mothers.

3. Wait a minute, Miranda. It's very cold outside. Here's your coat and hat.

   Here *is* your coat and hat? That won't fly. It should be this: Here <u>are</u> your coat and hat.

4. I see Robin and Kacey, but where's the other kids?

   Where *is* the other kids? No. I see Robin and Kacey, but where <u>are</u> the other kids?

5. Every player on the team played their best.

   *Every* is singular, *their* is plural. Here are two solutions:
   • Every player on the team played his/her best.
   • All the players on the team played their best.

6. Either Kate or Meg might lend me their bike.

   *Either* is singular, *their* is plural. Either Kate or Meg might lend me <u>her</u> bike.

7. During the scary part of the movie, we could all feel a lot of fear rushing through our body.

   How many people share this one body? During the scary part of the movie, we could all feel a lot of fear rushing through our <u>bodies</u>.

8. There's a lot of good reasons to learn the rules of proper writing.

   Now there's some bad writing! There <u>are</u> a lot of good reasons to learn the rules of proper writing.

9. I don't like these kind of movies.

   *These* is plural, *kind* is singular, and *movies* is plural. Both of these are correct:
   • I don't like this kind of movie.
   • I don't like these kinds of movies.

10. All the girls wore a dress to the dance.

    That must have been one huge dress! All the girls wore <u>dresses</u> to the dance.

# CHAPTER FOUR

# Words, Words, Words

plans on getting
you better - a lot
...insure you
use to see

# WACKY WORDS
## WE LOVE TO MISUSE

**Read this paragraph aloud:** I am sure that everyone of you all ready knows that spoken English and written English are sometimes very different than each other. What sounds fine to the ear sometimes looks weak, informal, or even dumb on paper. For example, we say "I should of eaten my veggies," but what we are suppose to write is this: "I should *have* eaten my veggies." We are so use to seeing and hearing certain words and phrases misused that we often don't even notice them when we proofread our papers. However, if you plan on getting A's on alot of your language arts papers, you better learn to spot these sorts of goofs. What are these sneaky, wacky words? Read on! I insure you that if you read this chapter, you will discover that their are quite a few words which you are misusing.

Did that paragraph sound fine to you? It probably did, but it was filled with wacky words—words we often use in speech and writing that are wrong. How many of these wacky words did you catch in that paragraph?

| This | should be this |
|------|----------------|
| everyone of you | every one of you |
| all ready knows | already knows |
| different than each other | different from each other |
| suppose to write | supposed to write |
| use to seeing | used to seeing |
| plan on getting A's | plan to get A's |
| alot | a lot |
| you better learn | you had better learn |
| I insure you | I assure you |
| their are | there are |
| which you are misusing | that you are misusing |

# A and An

Use *a* before words beginning with consonant sounds, even if that sound is made by a vowel. (Reminder: consonants are all the letters of the alphabet except *a, e, i, o, u,* and sometimes *y.*)

| | | |
|---|---|---|
| a bat | a hat | a cat |
| a university | a yo-yo | a 100-dollar bill |

Use *an* before words beginning with vowel sounds, even if that sound is made by a consonant. (Reminder: the vowels are *a, e, i, o, u,* and sometimes *y.*)

| | | |
|---|---|---|
| an oasis | an M&M | an honor (silent *h*) |
| an apple | an *F* | an hour (silent *h*) |

# Affect and Effect

These are two tricky words! Here is the key to using them correctly:

**EFFECT:**
> As a noun = the result or outcome of something
> If you don't wear your bicycle helmet, the <u>effect</u> could be very bad.

As a verb = to cause or to bring something into being
The teacher tried to <u>effect</u> a change in the students' study
  habits.

AFFECT:

As a noun = emotions (a very rarely used word except by
  psychologists)
The child's <u>affect</u> was very disturbed after she saw the
  scary movie.

As a verb = to influence something
The movie didn't <u>affect</u> me as much as it did my little sister.

## If it's a noun you need, always choose *effect* (unless you're a psychologist talking about emotions).

RIGHT:
Scary movies have a bad <u>effect</u> on many kids.

RIGHT:
My apology didn't have the <u>effect</u> I thought it would have.

## If it's a verb you need, *affect* is the right choice 90 percent of the time.

To be sure, substitute the words *cause* and *influence*, and see
which is better.

*Affect* = Influence
*Effect* = Cause

RIGHT:
Too much rainy weather <u>affects</u> [influences] my mood; it
  makes me grumpy.

RIGHT:
Too much rainy weather from the hurricane <u>effected</u>
  [caused] flooding and beach erosion.

# All right and [Alright]

WRONG:
It is not <u>alright</u> to write this way.

RIGHT:
It is <u>all</u> <u>right</u> to write this way.

### Caution—Major Mistake Territory

Believe it or not, there is no such word as *alright*. Yes, you see it often even in books and newspapers, but it's absolutely wrong.

# Almost and Most

Students often use *most* when *almost* is much better.

INFORMAL:
   Most <u>everybody</u> we invited showed up for the party.
BETTER:
   Almost <u>everybody</u> we invited showed up for the party.

# A lot and [Alot]

There is no such word as *alot*.

WRONG:
   This is a goof that students make <u>alot</u>.
RIGHT:
   This is a goof that students make <u>a</u> <u>lot</u>.

# Among and Between

Use *between* when there are two people or things involved; use *among* when there are more than two involved.

RIGHT:
   This is just <u>between</u> Lamar and me.
RIGHT:
   <u>Among</u> the three girls, Jocelyn runs the fastest.

Exception to the rule: when you're talking about differences, always use *between*.

**RIGHT:**
Do you know the difference <u>between</u> bees, wasps, and hornets?

# **A**mount and Number

*Amount* = how much (you can't count them)
*Number* = how many (you can count them)

**WRONG:**
A large <u>amount</u> <u>of</u> <u>kids</u> were absent from school today.

**RIGHT:**
A large <u>number</u> <u>of</u> <u>kids</u> were absent from school today because a large <u>amount</u> of <u>snow</u> fell during the night.

# **A**nd and To

Students often use the word *and* when the better word is *to*.

**INFORMAL:**
When you write papers, <u>try</u> <u>and</u> write right.

**BETTER:**
When you write papers, <u>try</u> <u>to</u> write right.

**INFORMAL:**
Be <u>sure</u> <u>and</u> study for the test.

**BETTER:**
Be <u>sure</u> <u>to</u> study for the test.

# **A**nyway and [Anyways]

*Anyways* is not a word.

179

<u>WRONG:</u>

I don't care if you ate all the chips; I didn't want them <u>anyways</u>.

<u>RIGHT:</u>

I don't care if you ate all the chips; I didn't want them <u>anyway</u>.

## Around and About

It is not absolutely wrong to use *around* to mean *approximately*, but it is very informal.

<u>INFORMAL:</u>

I am a heavyweight fighter, and I weigh <u>around</u> 240.

<u>BETTER:</u>

I am a heavyweight fighter. I weigh <u>about</u> 240 and I run <u>around</u> the house twenty times every night before bedtime.

# BRAIN TICKLERS
### Set # 13

Find the goofs in these sentences and correct them.

1. My sister is going to an university in Wyoming.

2. I don't like the affect that Nutrasweet has on me; if I drink several Diet Cokes, I get a whopping headache.

3. I used to do alright in math, but recently I don't like it alot.

4. Most all the kids on the tennis team are in eighth grade.

5. Who is the best gymnast between the three boys?

6. Please give me a large amount of apples.

7. I am around five feet tall.

8. Try and be here by noon.

(Answers are on page 204.)

Remember: Spoken English and written English (at least properly written formal English) are sometimes very different. Unless you are deliberately writing in a chatty, casual style, check your writing carefully for signs of informal English. Don't worry about sounding like a nerd. Formal English doesn't sound stuffy and weird—it sounds clear, clean, and strong.

# Behind and In back of

*In back of* is very informal.

**INFORMAL:**
Kristen, put your bicycle <u>in</u> <u>back</u> <u>of</u> the house.
**BETTER:**
Kristen, put your bicycle <u>behind</u> the house.

# Better and Had better

*You had better* is informal. *You better* is even more informal and looks very sloppy in formal writing.

**VERY INFORMAL:**
You <u>better</u> do your homework.
**INFORMAL:**
You <u>had</u> <u>better</u> do your homework.
**BETTER:**
You <u>should</u> do your homework.

# Bring and Take

*Bring* shows movement toward the speaker.
*Take* shows movement away from the speaker.

### WRONG:

As I ran out the door, Dad shouted, "Here, remember to <u>bring</u> your lunch with you to school."

### RIGHT:

As I ran out the door, Dad shouted, "Here, remember to <u>take</u> your lunch with you to school."

# By, Buy, and Bye

This is not tricky territory. Goofs made in this arena are care-lessness.

### WRONG:

Come <u>bye</u> my house and we'll go <u>by</u> some baseball cards. Until then, <u>buy</u>.

### RIGHT:

Come <u>by</u> my house and we'll go <u>buy</u> some baseball cards. Until then, <u>bye</u>.

# Can and May

*Can* = has the ability to do something
*May* = has permission to do something
*May* = might do something

### WRONG:

<u>Can</u> I have a hamburger, please?

### RIGHT:

<u>May</u> I have a hamburger, please?

### RIGHT:

Wesley <u>can</u> play baseball well. (He has the ability.)

### RIGHT:

Ryan <u>may</u> not play baseball until he has done his home-work. (He does not have permission.)

RIGHT:
>  Hartley <u>may</u> play baseball this spring, but he hasn't decided yet. (He might play baseball.)

# Different from and Different than

*Different from* is better when you're comparing two things, but *different than* is used when clauses follow.

(A clause is a group of words that contains a subject and a verb. See page 72 for more about clauses.)

COMPARISON:
>  Your shoes are different <u>from</u> mine.

COMPARISON:
>  This piece of chicken tastes different <u>from</u> that one.

WITH A CLAUSE:
>  This movie is different <u>than</u> I thought it would be.

WITH A CLAUSE:
>  This town looks a lot different <u>than</u> it did when I grew up here.

# Every place and Everywhere

These are very informal: *every place, some place, any place, no place.*

INFORMAL:
>  I've looked <u>every place</u> for my social studies book. There's <u>no place</u> left to look, but it must be <u>some place</u> around here.

BETTER:
>  I've looked <u>everywhere</u> for my social studies book. There's <u>nowhere</u> left to look, but it must be <u>somewhere</u> around here.

# Farther and Further

Use *farther* and *farthest* for distance.

>  I'm too tired to walk <u>farther</u>.
>  Kacey lives <u>farther</u> from my house than I thought.

Use *further* and *furthest* to mean longer or more.

> I want to study this <u>further</u>. (meaning longer or in more depth)
> This relationship can go no <u>further</u>. (meaning no longer)
> In Mexico, the dollar goes <u>further</u>. (meaning more money)

## Fewer and Less

If you can count them, use *fewer*. If you can't count them, use *less*.

<u>WRONG:</u>
> There are <u>less</u> kids here than I expected.

<u>RIGHT:</u>
> There are <u>fewer</u> kids here than I expected.
> (You can count kids.)

<u>RIGHT:</u>
> There has been <u>less</u> snow this year than last year, so we
> have <u>fewer</u> snow days to make up.
> (You can't count snow; you can count days.)

<u>RIGHT:</u>
> We have <u>less</u> milk, <u>less</u> flour, <u>fewer</u> grapes, <u>less</u> maple
> syrup, and <u>fewer</u> potatoes in our refrigerator than you
> have in yours.

## Foot and Feet

Many kids (and adults, too) use *foot* when *feet* is correct.

<u>WRONG:</u>
> The swimming pool is twelve <u>foot</u> deep.

<u>RIGHT:</u>
> The swimming pool is twelve <u>feet</u> deep.

<u>WRONG:</u>
> The lifeguard is six <u>foot</u> tall.

<u>RIGHT:</u>
> The lifeguard is six <u>feet</u> tall.

It is correct to use *foot* in compound adjectives (two-word adjectives) that come before the noun.

RIGHT:

I need four <u>10-foot</u> [compound adjective] boards [noun] of treated lumber.

RIGHT:

We have two <u>7-foot</u> [compound adjective] players [noun] on our basketball team.

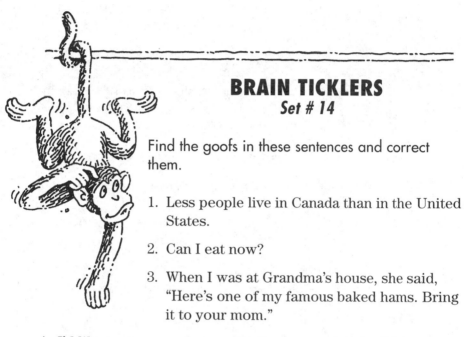

# BRAIN TICKLERS
## Set # 14

Find the goofs in these sentences and correct them.

1. Less people live in Canada than in the United States.

2. Can I eat now?

3. When I was at Grandma's house, she said, "Here's one of my famous baked hams. Bring it to your mom."

4. I'd like to go someplace really fun on our date tonight.

5. Mom said, "You better clean your room or you'll be grounded."

6. My prom dress is very different than Erica's.

7. I'm exhausted. I don't think I can swim one inch further.

8. The doctor says that, judging by my shoe size, I should be about six foot tall when I finish growing.

9. The bag of chips fell down in back of the refrigerator.

(Answers are on page 205.)

# Good and Well

*Good* is an adjective and *well* is an adverb.

If you remember that, you have the *good/well* problem licked.

Old Blue is a <u>good</u> dog. (adjective describing *dog*)
You've trained Old Blue <u>well</u>. (adverb describing *trained*)

This is a <u>good</u> salad. (adjective describing *salad*)
I can't taste the salad <u>well</u> because I have a cold. (adverb describing *taste*)

Remember linking verbs and action verbs? (See page 46.)

You <u>smell</u> <u>good</u>; that's a nice perfume. (*smell* is a linking verb)
Now that you took your cold medicine, you should be able to <u>smell</u> <u>well</u>. (*smell* is an action verb)

You <u>look</u> <u>good</u>. (*look* is a linking verb)
<u>Look</u> at this picture <u>well</u>. (*look* is an action verb)

Which is correct?

I'm over my cold and I feel <u>well</u>.
I'm over my cold and I feel <u>good</u>.

Both are correct. It is okay to use *well* as an adjective when you're talking about health.

# Have and Got

Notice how often you can get rid of the word *got*. Saying "I have got" is kind of silly, if you think about it, because "I have" says it all.

**INFORMAL:**
I haven't <u>got</u> enough money to buy the pet python I want.

BETTER:
> I don't <u>have</u> enough money to buy the pet python I want.

INFORMAL:
> I've <u>got</u> a lot of homework tonight.

BETTER:
> I <u>have</u> a lot of homework tonight.

INFORMAL:
> I have really <u>got</u> to study these wacky words for the wacky test tomorrow.

BETTER:
> I really <u>have</u> to study these wacky words for the wacky test tomorrow.

# Have and Of

The word *of* is often used when *have* is the correct word.

WRONG:
> If he would <u>of</u> listened to me, this never would <u>of</u> happened.

RIGHT:
> If he would <u>have</u> listened to me, this never would <u>have</u> happened.

BETTER:
> If he <u>had</u> listened to me, this never would have happened.

WRONG:
> I could <u>of</u> run that race faster. I should <u>of</u> tried harder.

RIGHT:
> I could <u>have</u> run that race faster. I should <u>have</u> tried harder.

WRONG:
> Elizabeth might <u>of</u> made the highest grade in the class.

RIGHT:
> Elizabeth might <u>have</u> made the highest grade in the class.

# How and That

*How* is often used as a conjunction when the correct word is *that*.

INFORMAL:
> Stop reminding me <u>how</u> I have more homework to do.

BETTER:

Stop reminding me <u>that</u> I have more homework to do.

INFORMAL:

Austin is complaining <u>how</u> there's not enough peach pie for him to have another piece.

BETTER:

Austin is complaining <u>that</u> there's not enough peach pie for him to have another piece.

# In and Into

*In* indicates where something is right now.
*Into* implies movement from one place to another.

INFORMAL:

Go <u>in</u> the house.

BETTER:

Go <u>into</u> the house.

INFORMAL:

Put the ice cream <u>in</u> the freezer.

BETTER:

Put the ice cream <u>into</u> the freezer.

RIGHT:

Mom yelled, "I am <u>in</u> the car waiting for you. If you don't get <u>into</u> the car right now, you're going to see tire tracks."

# Its and It's

*It's* is a contraction that is short for *it is* or *it has*—never use it for anything else.

> **WRONG:**
> Its absolutely amazing how often students make this mistake!
> **RIGHT:**
> It's even more amazing how often adults make this mistake!

> **WRONG:**
> Its time to eat. Its been a long time since I've eaten.
> **RIGHT:**
> It's time to eat. It's been a long time since I've eaten.

*Its* is possessive and shows that something owns or has something: its tail, its mother, its bark. Even though we write "the dog's tail" with an apostrophe, we write "its tail" without an apostrophe; *its* already implies possession and doesn't need an apostrophe.

> **WRONG:**
> Its cute how the puppy wags it's tail.
> **RIGHT:**
> It's cute how the puppy wags its tail.

# Like and As

*Like* is a preposition used to compare one thing to another. It means "similar to" or "for example."

> **RIGHT:**
> This flower looks like a rose.
> **RIGHT:**
> This tastes more like lemonade than limeade.
> **RIGHT:**
> You look like your mother.
> **RIGHT:**
> I'm good at racket sports like tennis and ping pong.

*As* and *as if* are conjunctions used before clauses.

(Reminder: a clause has a subject and a verb.)

INFORMAL:

I studied hard <u>like</u> I knew I should.

BETTER:

I studied hard <u>as</u> I knew I should.

INFORMAL:

You look <u>like</u> you've seen a ghost.

BETTER:

You look <u>as</u> <u>if</u> you've seen a ghost.

These formal sentences probably sound stuffy and awkward to you. The *like/as* rule is changing even in formal writing, but it's still important to be aware that the proper way to write is like I'm teaching you. (Did you catch that goof?)

The word *like* is used a lot these days as slang (see page 232) and as a filler word similar to *uh* and *well*.

VERY SLOPPY:

I like thought we could go like to a movie together.

MUCH BETTER:

I thought maybe we could go to a movie together.

## Like and That

Remember that *like* is used for comparisons—it is not a conjunction.

INFORMAL:

I feel <u>like</u> you should give me a raise in my allowance.

BETTER:

I feel <u>that</u> you should give me a raise in my allowance.

## Lose and Loose

This is just a spelling goof, but it's one you will see often.

WRONG:

The stone in my ring is <u>lose</u>. I surely don't want to <u>loose</u> it.

RIGHT:

The stone in my ring is <u>loose</u>. I surely don't want to <u>lose</u> it.

## Me and Myself

Some people think that saying *myself* sounds more polite than saying *me* or *I*. It doesn't—it just sounds wrong. Never use *myself* when *me* or *I* sounds right. (The same goes for *yourself*, *herself*, and *himself*.)

WRONG:
   Lateesha and <u>myself</u> were invited to the party.
RIGHT:
   Lateesha and <u>I</u> were invited to the party.

WRONG:
   Mom baked chocolate chip cookies for Eliza and <u>myself</u>.
RIGHT:
   Mom baked chocolate chip cookies for Eliza and <u>me</u>.

RIGHT:
   Tucker ate the chocolate chip cookies all by <u>himself</u>.
   (You wouldn't say "Tucker ate the cookies all by <u>him</u>.")
RIGHT:
   I hurt <u>myself</u>.
   (You wouldn't say "I hurt <u>me</u>.")

# BRAIN TICKLERS
### Set # 15

Find the goofs in these sentences and correct them.

1. I'll lend you my watch if you promise not to loose it.

2. Don't throw anything in the shark tank.

3. I cleaned up my room like my mom told me to.

4. Did I do good on that last exercise?

5. I feel like you're trying to bully me into giving you my last nacho.

6. Have you got any cash on you?

7. I've been thinking lately how I'd like to learn to play a musical instrument.

8. Meg and myself really appreciate your giving us a ride.

9. Pablo acted as a prince.

10. This is the end of this set of exercises. Its finished!

(Answers are on page 206.)

# Pair and Pairs

*Pair* is singular; *pairs* is plural.

**WRONG:**
We rented three <u>pair</u> of skis.
**RIGHT:**
We rented three <u>pairs</u> of skis.

# Plan on and Plan to

*Plan on* is very informal.

**INFORMAL:**
Do you <u>plan on going</u> to the football game?
**BETTER:**
Do you <u>plan to go</u> to the football game?

# Sit and Set

*Sit* means "to take a seat or sit down."

I want to <u>sit</u> here a while and rest.
<u>Sit</u> in the blue chair.

*Set* means "to place something."

Please <u>set</u> this blue chair in that corner.
<u>Set</u> the red cushion on the blue chair.

**WRONG:**

Miranda, why did you <u>sit</u> your grammar book on top of a hot stove when you knew it would catch fire?

**RIGHT:**

Miranda, why did you <u>set</u> your grammar book on top of a hot stove when you knew it would catch fire?

**WRONG:**

For that, Miranda, you must <u>set</u> in the corner for an hour and think about your poor, sad grammar book.

**RIGHT:**

For that, Miranda, you must <u>sit</u> in the corner for an hour and think about your poor, sad grammar book.

# Than and Then

Students often use the word *then* when they mean *than*.

*Than* is a conjunction. It links two parts of a sentence that are being compared to each other.

RIGHT:
My dog barks louder <u>than</u> your dog barks.

*Then* is an adverb telling when something happened.

RIGHT:
Kacey put away her toys, <u>then</u> crawled into bed and fell asleep.

WRONG:
I have more homework tonight <u>then</u> you do.

RIGHT:
I have more homework tonight <u>than</u> you do.

# This and A

*This* is a very overused word. It implies something right here, close at hand. Don't use *this* when the word *a* is better.

INFORMAL:
I bought <u>this</u> great new dress that I want to show you.

BETTER:
I bought <u>a</u> great new dress that I want to show you.

INFORMAL:
There's <u>this</u> new video game on the market that I'm dying to buy.

BETTER:
There's <u>a</u> new video game on the market that I'm dying to buy.

RIGHT:
Look at <u>this</u> splinter I got in my foot.

RIGHT:
Take <u>this</u> notebook with you to school.

# To, Too, and Two

Don't get too careless with your two's!

**WRONG:**

There are not <u>two</u> many possible ways <u>too</u> spell the number <u>to</u>.

**RIGHT:**

There are not <u>too</u> many possible ways <u>to</u> spell the number <u>two</u>.

# Waiting on and Waiting for

Unless you're talking about a waiter, waitress, or other person who is serving you, always use *waiting for*.

**INFORMAL:**

My mom is at home <u>waiting on</u> me to call her.

**BETTER:**

My mom is at home <u>waiting for</u> me to call her.

**RIGHT:**

The waitress is <u>waiting on</u> me.

# Which and That

*That* is the first word of a phrase or clause that is essential for the sentence to make sense or to mean what you want it to mean (see page 72 for more about phrases and clauses).

**RIGHT:**

The bike <u>that</u> I want for my birthday is a 21-speed blue mountain bike.

(I'm not talking about just any bike; I'm talking specifically about the one I want for my birthday. The clause "that I want for my birthday" tells exactly which bike I'm talking about. Without that clause, the sentence doesn't say what I mean.)

**DOESN'T SAY WHAT I MEAN:**

The bike is a 21-speed blue mountain bike.

*Which* is the first word of a phrase or clause that is not essential. If you can insert the words "by the way" and the sentence still means what you want it to mean, use *which*.

**RIGHT:**

My blue mountain bike, <u>which</u> I got for my birthday, has 21 speeds.

(The clause "which I got for my birthday" is a by-the-way clause. The information is not essential—I could leave it out and the sentence would still make sense.)

**DOES SAY WHAT I MEAN:**

My blue mountain bike has 21 speeds.

When the information is essential, use *that* and don't use commas. When the information is not essential, use *which* and do use commas.

**WRONG:**

The class, that I'm doing best in, is algebra.

("That I'm doing best in" is essential for the sentence to make sense.)

**RIGHT:**

The class that I'm doing best in is algebra.

**WRONG:**

My left foot that is slightly bigger than my right foot is the one I broke.

(The fact that my left foot is slightly bigger than my right foot is a by-the-way phrase. This information is not necessary in order for the sentence to make sense.)

**RIGHT:**

My left foot, which is slightly bigger than my right foot, is the one I broke.

(Notice the two commas that appear in this sentence. Commas come before and after by-the-way phrases.)

Check this out:

<u>RIGHT:</u>
Dad's pair of skis that I lost cost $200.
(This is correct if your dad has several pairs of skis and the specific pair you lost are the ones that cost $200. In this case, the information "that I lost" is essential in order to indicate which specific pair of skis you're talking about.)

<u>ALSO RIGHT:</u>
Dad's pair of skis, which I lost, cost $200.
(This is correct if Dad had only one pair of skis, they cost $200, and, by the way, you lost them. Notice the commas before and after the by-the-way clause.)

## Which and Who

Use *which* for things; use *who* for people.

<u>WRONG:</u>
My dad is the candidate <u>which</u> won the election.
<u>RIGHT:</u>
My dad is the candidate <u>who</u> won the election.

## Who and Whom

Writers get so confused over *who* and *whom* that they often give up and use *who* all the time. As a result, *whom* is about to die out of our language. There's really no reason to be afraid of *who* and *whom* because the trick for remembering which to use is quite easy. Here's the trick: when in doubt, substitute the words *he* and *him*. Notice which sounds better. If *he* is correct, use *who*. If *him* is correct, use *whom*.

I wonder (who/whom) will be at baseball practice today.
    Which sounds okay?
    • he will be at practice today—sounds okay
    • him will be at practice today—does not sound okay
<u>RIGHT:</u>
I wonder <u>who</u> will be at baseball practice today.

Never argue with the guy (who/whom) is wearing the umpire's suit!
Which sounds okay?
- he is wearing the suit—sounds okay
- him is wearing the suit—does not sound okay

RIGHT:
Never argue with the guy <u>who</u> is wearing the umpire's suit!

We all wondered (who/whom) the winner was.
Which sounds okay?
- he was the winner—sounds okay
- him was the winner—does not sound okay

RIGHT:
We all wondered <u>who</u> the winner was.

With (who/whom) are you going?
Which sounds okay?
- I'm going with he—does not sound okay
- I'm going with him—sounds okay

RIGHT:
With <u>whom</u> are you going?

(Who/Whom) is that for?
Which sounds okay?
- that is for he—does not sound okay
- that is for him—sounds okay

RIGHT:
<u>Whom</u> is that for?
(This might sound weird to you. We may not often speak
this way, but it's correct.)

# Why, How come, and What for

*How come* and *what for* are very informal.

INFORMAL:
<u>What</u> are you doing that <u>for</u>?
BETTER:
<u>Why</u> are you doing that?

**INFORMAL:**

<u>How come</u> you're not taking the bus to school?

**BETTER:**

<u>Why</u> are you not taking the bus to school?

# ONE WORD OR TWO?

## Many times students use one word when two words are needed.

Here's a clue for when the proper choice is two words: Can you put other words in the middle? If so, use two words.

**WRONG:**

We were *already* to leave.

**RIGHT:**

We were *all* [set and packed and] *ready* to leave.

**WRONG:**

I want pizza *everyday* for dinner.

**RIGHT:**

I want pizza *every* [single] *day* for dinner.

Each of these sentences is correct:

We were *all ready* to leave when we noticed that Leroy had *already* left.

Does *anyone* know whether *any one* of my friends is going to the dance?

*Sometime* in the future it is possible that we will be able to spend *some time* in Alaska.

*Everyone* knew that many kids had gone to the circus, and *every one* of them had a good time.

*Every day* I find myself getting upset by *everyday* problems like too much homework to do.

*Somebody* told the lifeguard that *some body*, probably a mouse or a rat, was floating in the swimming pool.

# CONFUSING PEARS

| | |
|---|---|
| Which word should I use? | Which word should I write? |
| or is it | or is it |
| Which word should I yews? | Which word should I right? |
| or is it | or is it |
| Which word should I you's? | Which word should I rite? |

It may knot seam fare, but their are dozens of confusing pears (and trios) of words in the English language, and writers often fowl up when using them. It happens all the thyme: we use won word when we mean another. We make word errors day and knight! Eye will give yew a peace of advice: reed your work carefully and bee alert four these sneaky critters. Goodness nose, I'd be embarrassed if I rote a paper with two many goofs! Aye no ewe wood bee two, sew hears sum aide from mi too yew.

Did you catch all these goofs?

| | | |
|---|---|---|
| knot—not | seam—seem | fare—fair |
| their—there | pears—pairs | fowl—foul |
| thyme—time | won—one | knight—night |
| eye—I | yew—you | peace—piece |
| reed—read | bee—be | four—for |
| nose—knows | rote—wrote | two—too |
| aye—I | no—know | ewe—you |

| | | |
|---|---|---|
| wood—would | bee—be | two—too |
| sew—so | hears—here's | sum—some |
| aide—aid | mi—me | too—to |
| yew—you | | |

Do you know when to use one word and when to use the other? Don't sweat it—even the pros often get confused. That's why the pros' favorite book is the dictionary.

Read this list, but don't try to memorize all these words. Enjoy the fun of two words masquerading as each other; words often completely change their meanings by altering only a letter or two. When you are even a bit unsure about the precise meaning of a word, look it up.

## Spelling Slip-Ups

| | |
|---|---|
| accept—except | envelope—envelop |
| advice—advise | forward—foreword |
| alter—altar | gig—jig |
| assure—ensure—insure | human—humane |
| bait—bate | hurdle—hurtle |
| born—borne | intense—intensive |
| breath—breathe | later—latter |
| capital—capitol | moral—morale |
| clinch—clench | personal—personnel |
| compliment—complement | principal—principle |
| confident—confidant | prophecy—prophesy |
| deadly—deathly | stationery—stationary |
| desert—dessert | track—tract |
| emigrate—immigrate | yea—yeah |
| eminent—imminent | |

# BRAIN TICKLERS
## Set # 16

Find the goofs in these sentences and correct them.

1. Mom bought me five new pair of knee socks in funky colors.

2. I use to go out with Brian, and I think he might of asked me to the dance if he weren't interested in Katie.

3. Bring everyone of your new video games when you come to my house.

4. Who are you going to the dance with?

5. Set down and rest a few minutes.

6. Marshall is one of my cousins which live in North Carolina.

7. My nose, that has been stuffy all spring, would appreciate a reduction in the pollen in the air.

8. Will your mom let you eat Hershey bars that contain sugar and chocolate?

9. This is a long reign.

10. What did you bring your racket for? It's snowing.

11. I had this really great idea for our science project that I told the teacher about.

12. Dad, don't leave yet—wait on me!

13. Do you plan on going water skiing today?

14. Its knot save two-holed you're breathe four to lawn—yew cud dye!

(Answers are on page 207.)

# BRAIN TICKLERS—
## THE ANSWERS

## Set # 13, page 180

1. My sister is going to an university in Wyoming.

   Even though *u* is a vowel, in this case it makes a consonant sound. My sister is going to <u>a</u> university in Wyoming.

2. I don't like the affect that Nutrasweet has on me; if I drink several Diet Cokes, I get a whopping headache.

   If it's a noun you need, usually use *effect*. I don't like the <u>effect</u> [meaning the result or outcome] that Nutrasweet has on me.

3. I used to do alright in math, but recently I don't like it alot.

   Two goofs! I used to do <u>all</u> <u>right</u> in math, but recently I don't like it <u>a</u> <u>lot</u>.

4. Most all the kids on the tennis team are in eighth grade.

   This is very informal. This is better: <u>Almost</u> all the kids on the tennis team are in eighth grade.

5. Who is the best gymnast between the three boys?

   There are three boys involved. Who is the best gymnast <u>among</u> the three boys?

6. Please give me a large amount of apples.

   You can count apples, so use *number*, not *amount*. Please give me a large <u>number</u> of apples.

7. I am around five feet tall.

   This sentence is very informal. This is better: I am <u>about</u> five feet tall.

8. Try and be here by noon.

   Very informal. To be more formal, write this: Try <u>to</u> be here by noon.

## Set # 14, page 185

1. Less people live in Canada than in the United States.

   You can count people, so use *fewer*, not *less*. <u>Fewer</u> people live in Canada than in the United States.

2. Can I eat now?

   Are you asking whether you have the ability or the permission? I assume you *can* eat now, unless your jaws are wired shut. If it's permission you're asking for, this is correct: <u>May</u> I eat now?

3. When I was at Grandma's house, she said, "Here's one of my famous baked hams. Bring it to your mom."

   *Bring* implies something coming toward the speaker. What Grandma meant to say was, "Here's one of my famous baked hams. <u>Take</u> it to your mom."

4. I'd like to go someplace really fun on our date tonight.

   Very informal. This is better: I'd like to go <u>somewhere</u> really fun on our date tonight.

5. Mom said, "You better clean your room or you'll be grounded."

   Mom had better clean up her sentence! This is better: Mom said, "You <u>had</u> better clean your room or you'll be grounded."

6. My prom dress is very different than Erica's.

   When you're comparing two things, use *different from*. My prom dress is very different <u>from</u> Erica's.

7. I'm exhausted. I don't think I can swim one inch further.

An inch is a measure of distance, so use *farther*. I don't think I can swim one inch <u>farther</u>.

8. The doctor says that, judging by my shoe size, I should be about six foot tall when I finish growing.

If you said that you are a six-foot boy, you'd be correct because the adjective *six-foot* comes before the noun *boy*. But in this case, this is correct: The doctor says that, judging by my shoe size, I should be about six <u>feet</u> tall when I finish growing.

9. The bag of chips fell down in back of the refrigerator.

*In back of* is very informal. This is better: The bag of chips fell down <u>behind</u> the refrigerator.

## Set # 15, page 192

1. I'll lend you my watch if you promise not to loose it.

There's that tricky loose/lose. I'll lend you my watch if you promise not to <u>lose</u> it.

2. Don't throw anything in the shark tank.

No problem! I don't have any intention of jumping into the tank and throwing sharks around. Oh, wait—I bet you mean this: Don't throw anything <u>into</u> the shark tank.

3. I cleaned up my room like my mom told me to.

Can you substitute *similar to*? (I cleaned up my room similar to my mom told me to.) No. In formal writing, it should be this: I cleaned up my room <u>as</u> my mom told me to.

4. Did I do good on that last exercise?

Yes, but you botched this one! It should be this: Did I do <u>well</u> [adverb describing the verb *do*] on that last exercise?

5. I feel like you're trying to bully me into giving you my last nacho.

   In formal English, *like* is not a conjunction. I feel <u>that</u> you're trying to bully me into giving you my last nacho.

6. Have you got any cash on you?

   Very informal. To be more formal, try this: <u>Do you have</u> any cash on you?

7. I've been thinking lately how I'd like to learn to play a musical instrument.

   This is better: I've been thinking lately <u>that</u> I'd like to learn to play a musical instrument.

8. Meg and myself really appreciate your giving us a ride.

   There's that sneaky *myself*. Who needs it? Meg and <u>I</u> really appreciate your giving us a ride.

9. Pablo acted as a prince.

   This is fine if you mean that Pablo played the role of a prince in a school play. But if you mean Pablo was a nice guy (comparing him to a prince), then say this: Pablo acted <u>like</u> a prince.

10. This is the end of this set of exercises. Its finished!

    Oh, no—not *that* goof. This is the end of this set of exercises. <u>It's</u> finished!

## Set # 16, page 203

1. Mom bought me five new pair of knee socks in funky colors.

   Saying *five pair* is like saying *five kid*. Mom bought me five new <u>pairs</u> of knee socks in funky colors.

2. I use to go out with Brian, and I think he might of asked me to the dance if he weren't interested in Katie.

Two goofs! I <u>used</u> to go out with Brian, and I think he might <u>have</u> asked me to the dance if he weren't interested in Katie.

3. Bring everyone of your new video games when you come to my house.

*Everyone* means "all the people." I think you mean every [single] one. Bring <u>every one</u> of your new video games when you come to my house.

4. Who are you going to the dance with?

Answer the question: I'm going to the dance with *him* (not *he*). If it's *him*, use *whom*.

**RIGHT:**
Whom are you going to the dance with?
**BETTER:**
With whom are you going to the dance?

5. Set down and rest a few minutes.

Set what down? My books? my grocery bags? my body? Oh, I bet you mean this: <u>Sit</u> down and rest a few minutes.

6. Marshall is one of my cousins which live in North Carolina.

Use *which* for things; use *who* for people. Marshall is one of my cousins <u>who</u> live in North Carolina.

7. My nose, that has been stuffy all spring, would appreciate a reduction in the pollen in the air.

*That has been stuffy all spring* is a by-the-way phrase. Obviously you have only one nose (don't you?), so we know which nose you're talking about, and the sentence makes sense without this phrase. By-the-way phrases, which are not absolutely necessary, begin with *which*. My nose, <u>which</u> has been stuffy all spring, would appreciate a reduction in the pollen in the air.

8. Will your mom let you eat Hershey bars that contain sugar and chocolate?

The wording of this sentence makes it sound as if some Hershey bars don't contain sugar and chocolate. I think you mean this: Will your mom let you eat Hershey bars, <u>which</u> contain sugar and chocolate?

9. This is a long reign.

   I assume you mean the reign of Queen Elizabeth, in which case this sentence is fine.
   - If you're talking about weather: This is a long <u>rain</u>.
   - If you're talking about horsy stuff: This is a long <u>rein</u>.

10. What did you bring your racket for? It's snowing.

    *What for* is very informal. This is better: <u>Why</u> did you bring your racket? It's snowing.

11. I had this really great idea for our science project that I told the teacher about.

    If you have a piece of paper in your hand with your great idea written on it, this sentence is fine (you're saying "*this* idea right here in my hand"). If not, try this: I had <u>a</u> really great idea for our science project that I told the teacher about.

12. Dad, don't leave yet—wait on me!

    Unless your dad is a waiter in a restaurant (or unless you usually treat your dad as if he's your servant), I think you mean this: Dad, don't leave yet—wait <u>for</u> me!

13. Do you plan on going water skiing today?

    *Plan on* is very informal. This is better: Do you <u>plan to go</u> water skiing today?

14. Its knot save two-holed you're breathe four to lawn—yew cud dye!

    Yes, all these words are spelled correctly, but wacky words often look or sound like other words. Perhaps what you mean is this: It's not safe to hold your breath for too long—you could die!

# CHAPTER FIVE

# Editing

# THE TOP GOOFS
# IN STUDENTS' WRITING

## What is the difference between the way students write and the way professionals write?

Easy question—here is the difference:

> Average student: write it, hand it in
>
> Above-average student: write it, edit it, rewrite it, hand it in
>
> Exceptional student: write it, edit it, rewrite it, edit it, rewrite it, hand it in
>
> Professional writer: write it, edit it, rewrite it, edit it, rewrite it, edit it, rewrite it, edit it, rewrite it, edit it, rewrite it, hand it in

Good writing is 20 percent inspiration and 80 percent cleanup. Learning the art of cleanup is just as important as learning the art of writing.

This chapter is not a set of rules; it's a set of reminders. Promise that you won't try to memorize anything in this chapter. If you want to memorize semicolon rules, go right ahead. But don't memorize from this page forward.

The reminders in this chapter are mainly for use when you edit your words, but they shouldn't cramp your style while you're writing. Your writing is like your room. Trash it all you want for the sake of expressing yourself; then when you clean it up, you will have something wonderfully unique to enjoy and to share with other people.

## Double talk

### Repeating repeating yourself yourself

**DOUBLE TALK:**
The day was unforgettable. I will never forget it.

**BETTER:**
The day was unforgettable.

**DOUBLE TALK:**

> I woke up about midnight because of a loud sound that woke me up.

**BETTER:**

> I woke up about midnight because of a loud sound.

**DOUBLE TALK:**

> I want apple pie à la mode with ice cream.

**BETTER:**

> I want apple pie à la mode.

**ALSO GOOD:**

> I want apple pie with ice cream.

## How can you avoid double talk in your writing?

**DOUBLE TALK:**

> It's simple: don't repeat the same thing <u>over and over</u> again. (Over and over? Why not over and over and over and over and over?)

**MORE DOUBLE TALK:**

> Don't repeat the same thing <u>over again</u>. (*Over* and *again* mean the same thing.)

**MORE DOUBLE TALK:**

> Don't <u>repeat</u> the same thing <u>again</u>. (The word *repeat* means "to say something again.")

**MORE DOUBLE TALK:**

> Don't <u>repeat the same thing</u>. (What else are you going to repeat—a different thing? If so, you wouldn't be repeating.)

**RIGHT AT LAST:**

> Don't repeat.

I know some of these sentences sound just fine, but that doesn't mean they *read* just fine. In conversation, we double-talk lots and lots (did you catch that one?). When we write, precision is power, and double talk is puny.

Listening for double talk can be fun. Many expressions we use in everyday speech are redundant. Check these out:

## Seeing Double

| | | |
|---|---|---|
| first time ever | unexpected surprise | right beside |
| separate out | rarely ever | free gift |
| mutual cooperation | 100% unanimous | small in size |
| 9 P.M. in the evening | each and every one | red in color |
| return again | original founder | square in shape |
| general consensus | important essentials | most unique |
| etc. etc. | so forth and so on | really truly |
| completely destroyed | one and the same | satisfactory enough |
| well off financially | first start | grateful thanks |
| revert back | end result | new innovation |
| personal friend | local resident | sum total |
| usual customs | tuna fish | whole wide world |
| stalling for time | other alternative | few in number |
| mix together | rise up | the reason is because |
| rock back and forth | this point in time | the reason why |
| month of June | over and done with | reserved exclusively |
| advance warning | continue on | circulate around |
| true fact | untrue lie | in this day and time |
| equally as important | extra additions | regular routine |
| may possibly | two polar opposites | final outcome |

# Excess baggage—unnecessary words

## We often pad our sentences with words that are obvious and unnecessary.

When we speak, these words aren't earsores, but when we write, they are eyesores. They clutter our writing, making it unclear, rambling, and sloppy. When you proofread, be ruthless: slash words that don't need to be there.

WEAK:
> I am sitting down on the chair.
> (Where else would you sit—up?)

BETTER:
> I am sitting on the chair.

WEAK:
> I am diving down into the water.
> (Do people ever dive sideways?)

BETTER:
> I am diving into the water.

WEAK:
> Will you please go and get my pencil for me?

STILL WEAK:
> Will you please go get my pencil for me?

BETTER:
> Will you please get my pencil for me?

WEAK:
> I ate dinner, then I watched TV, and then I went to bed.

BETTER:
> I ate dinner, watched TV, and went to bed.

WRONG:
> I needed a new book bag, and so my mom took me to
> buy one.
> (*And* and *so* are both conjunctions—you need only one.)

RIGHT:
> I needed a new book bag, and my mom took me to buy one.

WEAK:
> I finished my homework, so then I had time to play.

BETTER:
> I finished my homework, so I had time to play.

ALSO GOOD:
> I finished my homework; then I had time to play.

## Check out these unnecessary words:

> I cleaned up all <u>of</u> my stuff.
> This is some kind of <u>a</u> zebra, but I can't remember its name.
> The doctor stitched <u>up</u> my cut.
> I ate <u>a</u> half <u>of</u> my apple.
> We're <u>all</u> out of toothpaste.
> Put the dog outside <u>of</u> the house and bring the cat inside
> <u>of</u> the house.
> I can't decide whether <u>or</u> <u>not</u> to go to the game.

I opened <u>up</u> my birthday gift before my birthday.

Robin admitted <u>to</u> hiding his sister's Barbie doll.

We have a tennis court reserved <u>up</u> until 6:00.

It would be better to eat a healthy meal before the tennis match <u>rather</u> than to load up on junk.

I don't have anything <u>that</u> special to wear to the prom.

It snowed all night <u>long</u>.

My parents haven't given me my birthday present <u>as of</u> yet.

When you finish <u>up</u> your work, you may go <u>out</u> to the party. By the way, where is the party <u>at</u>?

I want to improve my writing, <u>and</u> yet I <u>just</u> love to throw extra, <u>unnecessary</u> words into sentences <u>at</u> every chance I get!

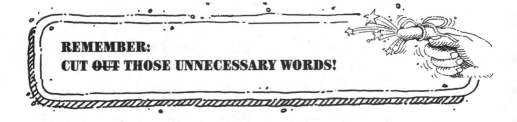

**REMEMBER:**
**CUT ~~OUT~~ THOSE UNNECESSARY WORDS!**

# Blah blah blah— enough words to drown a fish

## Good writing is crisp and clean.

"Garbage words" distract your readers, bore them, and confuse them. Long sentences are not necessarily a sign of intelligence; in fact, they are often a sign of sloppy writing. When you write, remember the KISS technique: Keep It Short and Simple.

Believe it or not, some professional writers are paid by the word; 20 cents a word is not uncommon, so *blah blah blah* could be worth 60 cents. Unfortunately, your language arts teacher will not hand you cash for padding your papers with a bunch of garbage words, so you might as well KISS.

**BLAH BLAH BLAH:**

At this point in time I really think that I need to start getting more of some kind of physical exercise.

**CRISP:**

I need to exercise more.

**BLAH BLAH BLAH:**

The reason why I left the door unlocked is because I was of the opinion that in the event that Dad got home during the time that I was out, he would be mad due to the fact that the door was locked.

**CRISP:**

I left the door unlocked because I thought Dad would be mad if he got home while I was out and found the door locked.

**BLAH BLAH BLAH:**

There are times in this day and age when I really feel very strongly that we should give more assistance to those who are currently homeless and have no place to live.

**CRISP:**

I often feel strongly that we should assist the homeless more than we do.

**BLAH BLAH BLAH:**

There are some people who cannot help using a lot of un-necessary words and excessive verbiage when they speak.

**CRISP:**

Some people cannot help being wordy when they speak.

| Who needs all these words | when you can say this? |
|---|---|
| at that point in time | then |
| ahead of schedule | early |
| I am in possession of | I have |
| in advance of | before |
| made an escape | escaped |

| | |
|---|---|
| it is my opinion that | I think |
| all of a sudden | suddenly |
| until such time as | until |
| in the event that | if |
| provided that | if |
| on the condition that | if |
| at a later date | later |
| due to the fact that | because |
| the reason why is that | because |
| owing to the fact that | since |
| had occasion to be | was |
| take into consideration | consider |
| did not pay attention to | ignored |
| as a matter of fact | in fact |
| in spite of the fact that | although |
| there is no doubt but that | no doubt |
| first of all | first |
| during the time that | while |

# What about me?
## Words that feel left out

I have encouraged you to delete words that you don't need.
Now I'm going to tell you not to leave out words you do need.

What would you think if your girlfriend or boyfriend said, "I like ice cream better than you"? You should definitely ask her or him to fill in the left-out words! Which does this mean:

- I like ice cream better than you like ice cream?
- I like ice cream better than I like you?

**WRONG:**
Mr. Jones, the physics teacher, called a meeting for students who hate physics and their parents.
(Anything else the students hate besides physics and their parents? Maybe squash or beets?)
**RIGHT:**
Mr. Jones, the physics teacher, called a meeting for students who hate physics and <u>for</u> their parents.

**WRONG:**
Is this movie similar or different from the last one you saw?
**RIGHT:**
Is this movie similar <u>to</u> or different from the last one you saw?

**WRONG:**
He had been loud in class and gotten into a lot of trouble.
**RIGHT:**
He had been loud in class and <u>had</u> gotten into a lot of trouble.

**WRONG:**
Parker is as tall, if not taller than, Ryan.
**RIGHT:**
Parker is as tall <u>as</u>, if not taller than, Ryan.

**WRONG:**
The mountains of Colorado are taller than Utah.
**RIGHT:**
The mountains of Colorado are taller than <u>those in</u> Utah.

**CONFUSING:**
I went to the circus with my cousin and friend.
(Is this one person or two?)
**IF YOU MEAN ONE PERSON:**
I went to the circus with Emily, my cousin and friend.
**IF YOU MEAN TWO PEOPLE:**
I went to the circus with my cousin and my friend.

# The weaklings—puny words

## Don't water down your writing with trite words.

We overuse many words and phrases in everyday speech, and they've become hackneyed, banal, and vapid. *Vapid* —now there's a great word! It means "lacking taste, zest, or flavor; flat, stale, dull, or tedious"—all the ways you don't want your writing to sound. Search your writing for weaklings and substitute a juicy word, something with a little flair or pizzazz.

PUNY:
> That's cool.

PIZZAZZ:
> That's wonderful; that's fascinating; that's exciting.

MEGA-PUNY (WRITING DOESN'T GET MUCH WEAKER THAN THIS):
> I wanted Craig to ask me to the prom so bad. It would've been real neat if he had, but, oh, well, he didn't. I went with Sam and we had a pretty nice time. You know, sometimes this sort of stuff turns out okay.

PIZZAZZ:
> I wanted Craig to ask me to the prom. I waited eagerly for his call, but it never came. I went with Sam instead, and we had a great time together. Sometimes things work out well even when you expect disaster.
>
> (Don't worry—no one is asking you to talk this way, but written language is different from spoken language.)

Get tough with the weaklings—use some power-packed words:

| Weak | Powerful |
|------|----------|
| real pretty | beautiful |
| so much | extremely |
| real cute | adorable |
| kind of nice | acceptable |
| pretty funny | odd |
| not so great | disappointing |
| a whole lot | a great deal |
| real mad | furious |
| so good | wonderful |
| pretty weak | frail |
| so bad | terrible |
| kind of bummed | depressed |
| real boring | dull |
| lots of | many |

## BRAIN TICKLERS
### Set # 17

Find the goofs in these sentences and correct them.

1. Bring your rollerblades with you when you come to my house.

2. I rarely ever sleep late, but today I stayed in bed until noon.

3. Dad's new car is a blue Ford with a black interior, with power steering and power brakes, and with an engine with six cylinders.

4. There are some people who pad their sentences with unnecessary words.

5. I got a flu shot yesterday. This is supposed to keep me from getting sick this winter.

6. That movie is so cool; you'll just love it.

7. I am sort of tired.

8. I like Bill better than Frank.

9. I know you want to go ice skating. I also want to go ice skating, too.

10. It has seldom been the case that I have vacuumed my room without Mom's prodding me.

11. There are many reasons why you should eat plenty of vegetables.

12. I need to get me something to eat.

13. I have never and probably will never be a brave bungee jumper.

14. Pat is smarter than all the boys in the class.

15. The reason I did poorly on the test is because my dog ate my study sheets.

(Answers are on page 253.)

# Undernourished phrases

## Vitamin therapy for your sentences

*This is a sentence.* It is grammatically correct and the punctuation is flawless. Do those facts make it a good sentence? Hardly. "This is a sentence" doesn't tell your reader anything very interesting. Check your writing for flat, dull, information-less sentences and give them a little nourishment. Don't add unnecessary filler words—add words power-packed with vitamins.

**UNDERNOURISHED:**
The kids quickly ate some food.

**WITH SOME VITAMINS:**
The boys quickly ate subs.

**MORE VITAMINS:**
The six boys quickly ate several foot-long subs.

**MORE VITAMINS:**
The six members of the boys' tennis team hungrily devoured several foot-long subs.

**MORE VITAMINS:**
The six members of the boys' tennis team hungrily devoured several foot-long subs after their tournament victory.

**MEGA-VITAMINS:**
Immediately after winning the regional tournament, the six members of the boys' tennis team hungrily devoured several foot-long subs, which David's mom had brought as a surprise.

**UNDERNOURISHED:**
A ball broke the neighbors' window.

**WITH SOME VITAMINS:**
A baseball accidentally broke the neighbors' window.

**MORE VITAMINS:**
A baseball, which Wesley accidentally hit toward the neighbors' house, broke their window.

**MORE VITAMINS:**
> A baseball, which Wesley accidentally hit toward the neighbors' house, shattered their kitchen window.

**MEGA-VITAMINS:**
> Wesley's wild hit, which he accidentally slammed toward the neighbors' house, shattered their kitchen window.

# Vague and foggy writing

## Don't be a chicken!

If you like to write on foggy days, go right ahead, but please edit your work before anyone else reads it. Unless you provide your reader with special fog-clearing goggles, nobody will understand what you're trying to say.

**FOGGY:**
> These issues are sometimes related to other issues, and maybe there is a connection between all the things we've been talking about. You see, these are important questions that have been raised, and in the future somebody ought to answer them.

**EXPLAIN YOURSELF:**
> These issues [what issues?] are sometimes [when?] related to [related in what ways?] other issues [what other issues?], and maybe [is there or isn't there?] there is a connection [what kind of connection?] between all the things [what things?] we've been talking about. You see [no, I certainly don't], these are important questions [what questions?] that have been raised [by whom?], and in the future [that's a very long time] somebody [who?] ought to [why ought they?] answer [how?] them.

**FOGGY:**
> I am not really convinced that the jury's ideas were entirely fair. I think maybe he should have gotten off easier and maybe he didn't do it anyway because it's possible he was innocent.

225

(Did the jury express ideas or was it a conviction? How much easier should he have gotten off? *Really, entirely, maybe, anyway, possible*—with each word, the fog gets thicker.)

**CLEAR:**

I am not convinced that the defendant was guilty in spite of the jury's verdict.

Foggy writing is a dead giveaway: you're either a bluffer or a chicken. Either you don't know what you're talking about or you're too shy to assert yourself. Have courage—say what you want to say!

# Double negatives

## This is a no-no, so don't-don't!

**WRONG:**

You <u>don't</u> have <u>no</u> business using two negatives in the same phrase. I <u>hardly</u> <u>never</u> make the double negative mistake, but when I do, my embarrassment is <u>unlike</u> <u>none</u> other.

**RIGHT:**

You <u>don't</u> have <u>any</u> business using two negatives in the same phrase. I <u>hardly</u> <u>ever</u> make the double negative mistake, but when I do, my embarrassment is <u>like</u> <u>none</u> other.

**WRONG:**

I haven't seen no two-toed sloths around here lately.

**RIGHT:**

I haven't seen any two-toed sloths around here lately.

These are obvious negatives—the *N*-words:

*no, none, nobody, nowhere, nothing, no one, never, not,* and words ending with *-n't* such as *can't, don't,* and *wouldn't*

These negatives are a little less obvious:

*hardly, scarcely, barely, rarely, unlike*

**WRONG:**
I don't see hardly any mess in my room.
**RIGHT:**
I see hardly any mess in my room.
**ALSO RIGHT:**
I don't see much mess in my room.

Check this out: double negatives actually cancel each other out!

I didn't eat no pizza = I did eat some pizza.
I hardly saw nothing = I did see something.
I don't want no trouble from you = I want some trouble from you.

Some sentences can contain more than one negative word and be correct. Usually, however, these sentences sound clumsy or confusing. Re-write them to make them clear.

**RIGHT:**
At <u>no</u> time did I know <u>nobody</u> in the room.
**BETTER:**
At all times I knew somebody in the room.

**RIGHT:**
I <u>don't</u> want to keep going in circles getting <u>nowhere</u>.
**BETTER:**
I want to stop going in circles and start making progress.

**RIGHT:**
It is <u>unlike</u> you to <u>never</u> speak up in class.
**BETTER:**
It is unlike you to be silent in class.

# Run-ons—sentences that go on and on and on and on and on and on and on and on and on and on and on . . .

## Run-on sentences are very hard for your reader to understand.

When one idea is complete, use a period. When a short group of thoughts or ideas is complete, end the paragraph and start a new one.

> Sometimes when a sentence gets revved up, it's hard for the writer to know when to stop because many ideas are bubbling to the surface, and all the ideas seem related to each other and, therefore, appropriate to be included in the same sentence, and the sentence ends up going on and on . . . and on and on for what seems like forever so that, meanwhile, the poor, unsuspecting reader has almost no idea what's happening, can't remember what was happening at the beginning of the sentence, can't foresee where all this is leading, and wonders if maybe the writer's computer has a jammed period key and that's why there's never an end to the world's longest (and the universe's second most confusing) sentence, and it would be the universe's most confusing except for this, which actually is the longest and most confusing sentence in the annals of history: Once upon a time long ago in the land of ridiculously long sentences . . .

> *Help! Please stop!*
> *This type of writing is guaranteed to*
> *drive your readers crazy!*

# Goofy goofs—misplaced phrases

## As you proofread, notice where you have placed descriptive phrases.

Phrases should usually be placed very close to the part of the sentence they describe. Careful proofreading can spare you some very embarrassing—and sometimes very funny—goofs.

**GOOFY:**

Lying in the grass on a warm day, the sun shone above me. (The phrase *lying in the grass on a warm day* comes closer to the noun *sun* than it does to the pronoun *me*. It sounds as though the sentence means this: The sun, which was lying in the grass on a warm day, shone above me.)

**MUCH BETTER:**

Lying in the grass on a warm day, I saw the sun shining above me.

**GOOFY:**

Three bicycles were reported stolen by the police yesterday. (The phrase *by the police* comes right after the word *stolen*. It sounds as though you just can't trust those police!)

**MUCH BETTER:**

The police reported that three bicycles were stolen yesterday.

**GOOFY:**

After being baked for 30 minutes, you should let the brownies cool.
(How do you taste when baked?)

**MUCH BETTER:**

After being baked for 30 minutes, the brownies should be allowed to cool.

**ALSO GOOD:**

After the brownies are baked for 30 minutes, let them cool.

**GOOFY:**

After years of neglect in a basement closet, I found my old teddy bear and brought it to my room.
(I feel sorry for you. All those years in a basement closet must have been rough for you.)

**MUCH BETTER:**

I found my old teddy bear, which had been neglected for years in a basement closet, and brought it to my room.

**GOOFY:**

Skiing on a cold, snowy day, icicles began to form on my
eyelashes.
(Icicles on skis? I'd like to see that.)

**MUCH BETTER:**

Skiing on a cold, snowy day, I noticed icicles beginning to
form on my eyelashes.

**GOOFY:**

Miranda ran to the teacher screaming her head off.
(I wonder what the teacher was so upset about.)

**MUCH BETTER:**

Miranda, screaming her head off, ran to the teacher.

**GOOFY:**

Having gashed his arm on the broken bottle, the doctor
sewed Josh's wounds.
(Did the doctor gash Josh's arm? That's not very nice. Or
did the doctor gash his own arm and then sew up Josh?
That's not very smart!)

**MUCH BETTER:**

The doctor sewed the wounds Josh had received from
gashing his arm on the broken bottle.

GOOFY:

With their cute, little, furry bodies, people adore golden retriever puppies.

(Not many people I know have cute, little, furry bodies.)

MUCH BETTER:

People adore golden retriever puppies' cute, little,
furry bodies.


# Slang

## That be cool writing, dude.

Dear Mr. Sutton,

Thank you very much for your generous offer of two
tickets to the Duke/Carolina basketball game, which I ac-
cept with gratitude and excitement. I look forward to wit-
nessing a Tarheel victory!

I send my best wishes to you and your family.

Sincerely,
Joshua Zinn


Hey, Bro!

Thanks, dude! Awesome! What a cool offer. I was like
yes when I got your message. I was going to spaz out if I
couldn't see that game, but now I'm major pumped. I can't
wait to watch our boys dog them Dookies.

Come over to my crib sometime soon and we'll hang
and chill a while then grab some grub.

Later,
Z


Is slang in or out? Is it rad or bad? It depends on what you are
writing and who will read it. If you wrote the first letter to your
best friend, you would sound like a nerd. If you wrote the second letter to your boss, you would probably be fired. Slang is
awesome in its place. Out of place, it makes your writing sound
silly, dumb, or disrespectful.

> ## WITH SLANG, WHEN IN DOUBT, CUT IT OUT.

# BRAIN TICKLERS
### Set # 18

Find the goofs in these sentences and correct them.

1. The doctor said that if I don't start eating something other than Hershey bars within a month my brain will be solid chocolate.

2. That movie is unlike none other I've seen.

3. I have never thought of myself as a nobody accomplishing nothing in life.

4. I went to visit my cousin in Atlanta because my parents were going on a trip to California, a trip they had looked forward to for a long time, and my cousin and I, along with several of her friends, had a great time shopping, seeing movies, and doing other things, like water skiing and snorkcling, that I had wanted to do for a long time but hadn't had a chance to do because my parents said it was more important for me to focus on school work, especially on improving my writing skills.

5. Ryan led his pet alligator, holding his head high with pride, into the winner's circle at the pet show.

6. Teresa watched the lion approach wide-eyed with fear.

7. Johnny is so sleepy he doesn't hardly remember his own name.

8. I told my mom I wanted to go to the mall to buy some supplies for my science project, and that is what happened.

9. I said a few nasty things to my parents that I'm not proud of.

10. Mom served dessert to my friends on paper plates.

11. I like your dress.

12. I think that maybe we should do something to improve the conditions of some people who are in some sort of trouble.

13. Man, we're really cooking now!

(Answers are on page 256.)

## Keeping everything consistent— parallel construction

### Have you heard the old saying about changing horses in midstream?

Picture it in your mind—crossing a stream on horseback and changing horses halfway across. Not a good idea. You're wondering what this has to do with writing a language arts paper? I'll show you. This is how it looks when you change ideas in mid sentence:

INCONSISTENT:
   I like playing baseball, reading about sports, and tacos.
      playing baseball = gerund phrase
      reading about sports = gerund phrase
      tacos = noun

CONSISTENT:
   I like playing baseball, reading about sports, and eating tacos.
      playing baseball = gerund phrase
      reading about sports = gerund phrase
      eating tacos = gerund phrase

**INCONSISTENT:**

We're studying equations, all about Europe, and to write well.

> equations = noun
> all about Europe = prepositional phrase
> to write well = infinitive phrase

**CONSISTENT:**

We're studying equations, European history, and writing techniques.

> equations = noun
> history = noun
> techniques = noun

**INCONSISTENT:**

Sally swung the bat and the ball was hit.

> Sally swung = active voice
> the ball was hit = passive voice

**CONSISTENT:**

Sally swung the bat and hit the ball.

> Sally swung = active voice
> (Sally) hit = active voice

**INCONSISTENT:**

It is better to do your homework early in the evening than waiting until you're sleepy.

**CONSISTENT:**

It is better to do your homework early in the evening than to wait until you're sleepy.

**INCONSISTENT:**

I invited my cousin, Parker Stevens; my friend, Ryan Hsu; and Marshall.

**CONSISTENT:**

I invited my cousin, Parker Stevens; my friend, Ryan Hsu; and my neighbor, Marshall Sutton.

Keeping it consistent also applies to the format of your writing. Notice how this section has been formatted.

- INCONSISTENT always comes before CONSISTENT.
- INCONSISTENT and CONSISTENT are always in capital letters.
- There is a colon after each INCONSISTENT and each CONSISTENT.
- The indentations are all the same.
- There is one line skipped between each pair of examples.

I could have formatted this page many different ways, but once I picked a style, I stuck with it. That's consistency—and it makes for easier reading. How might this page have looked if I had not been consistent? Here is the same example written two different ways—you decide which is easier to read.

inconsistent: Hartley says yes, Ryan says no, and Wesley said maybe. This is INCONSISTENT because it mixes verb tenses. Consistent: Hartley says yes, Ryan says no, and Wesley says maybe. Of course, it would also be consistent and correct to write it this way: Hartley says, "Yes," Ryan says, "No," and Wesley says, "Maybe."

**INCONSISTENT:**

Hartley says yes, Ryan says no, and Wesley said maybe. (This is inconsistent because it mixes verb tenses.)

**CONSISTENT:**

Hartley says yes, Ryan says no, and Wesley says maybe.

**ALSO CORRECT:**

Hartley says, "Yes," Ryan says, "No," and Wesley says, "Maybe."

# Get smart—powering up your brain cells

## When editing sentences, a writer must also edit his/her logic.

Get tough and ask yourself, does this make good sense? Does it make *any* sense?

### I DON'T THINK SO:
I want to see what you have to say.
(Do you know many people who hear with their eyes?)
### NOW YOU'RE THINKING:
I want to hear what you have to say.

### I DON'T THINK SO:
The hundred-year-old man rode his hundred-year-old horse down the hundred-year-old road to his cabin.
(Check with a vet—how many horses live to the age of 100?)
### NOW YOU'RE THINKING:
The hundred-year-old man rode his feeble, old horse down the hundred-year-old road to his cabin.

### I DON'T THINK SO:
The pirates sailed all seven continents seeking treasure.
(They must have had awesome ships if they could sail on land!)
### NOW YOU'RE THINKING:
The pirates sailed all four oceans seeking treasure.

### I DON'T THINK SO:
In our city, 80 percent of the children go to public school, 30 percent go to private school, and 3 percent are home schooled.

(Let's see, 80 percent + 30 percent + 3 percent = 113 percent. That's a lot of kids!)

NOW YOU'RE THINKING:

In our city, 80 percent of the children go to public school, 18 percent go to private school, and 2 percent are home schooled.

# Chop chop chop

## Tasteless bites vs. delicious sentences

Choppy sentences and paragraphs are dull and boring. Don't make sentences so short they sound like a two-year-old learning to talk. And don't use one-sentence paragraphs except for very strong emphasis. If you have only one sentence, weave that sentence into another paragraph.

BORING:

It's raining. It's cloudy, too. It's cold outside. I wish I had my raincoat with me.

BETTER:

It's cold, cloudy, and rainy outside, and I wish I had my raincoat with me.

BORING:

My cat's name is Boris. My dog's name is Bowser. My hamster's name is Sunny. My boa constrictor's name is Tough Stuff. I have four pets. Those are my pets.

BETTER:

I have four pets: a cat named Boris, a dog named Bowser, a hamster named Sunny, and a boa constrictor named Tough Stuff.

EVEN BETTER:

I have four great pets! Boris the cat gets along great with Bowser the dog, but Sunny the hamster stays as far away as possible from Tough Stuff the boa constrictor.

BORING:

I wanted to go to the store. My mom took me to the store. I saw a new video game there. I wanted the game. My mom let me buy it. I was happy. This paragraph is about as exciting as soggy cereal.

**BETTER:**

I wanted to go to the store, so my mom took me. I saw a new video game there that I wanted, and my mom let me buy it. I was happy, and this paragraph is a little better. But not much.

**EVEN BETTER:**

I heard about a great new video game from a friend, and I was excited to see it for myself. My mom was busy, but I sweet-talked her into taking me to the store. When I actually played the game on the store's demo system, it was far better than I had expected, and, believe it or not, my mom agreed to get it for me. I was ecstatic and, best of all, on the drive home Mom taught me to write paragraphs that don't remind my readers of soggy cereal.

What makes this last example strong? It contains an interesting mixture of sentence types: short and long, simple and more complex. If your writing sounds dull to you, you can be sure it will sound even duller to your reader. Spice it up with interesting words, varied sentence lengths, different styles of sentences, and points of emphasis.

# Repetition

## Can't you think of another word?

**REPETITIVE:**

It was a dark and stormy night. During the night, I had a nightmare about storms. I saw dark thunderclouds and lightning all night in my dreams. When I woke, my emotions were dark. It had been a very stormy night for me.

If a dictionary is the writer's best friend, a thesaurus is his or her second-best friend. The English language is too full of interesting words to keep using the same ones until your reader is bored to tears. For example:

Dark = unlit, dismal, dim, gloomy, murky, blurred, shadowy, cloudy, black, dusky

Stormy = fierce, inclement, turbulent, blustering,
   tumultuous
Night = evening, twilight, darkness

### MUCH BETTER:

It was a dark and blustering evening. As I slept, I had a
nightmare about storms. I saw murky thunderclouds and
lightning in my dreams. When I woke, my emotions were
gloomy. It had been a very tumultuous night for me.

Sometimes repetition works. If the writer uses it skillfully, repetition creates emphasis.

We have nothing to fear but fear itself.
Beauty is as beauty does.
. . . of the people, by the people, for the people

More often, repetition makes a sentence sound dumb or downright wacky.

### WACKY:

One thing that I would like to do would be to maybe be
a pilot.

### BETTER:

I might like to be a pilot.

### WACKY:

Emily told me that she thought that what that noise was
was thunder that was so loud that it was deafening, and I
think that she was right—that that was what it was.

BETTER:

Emily told me she thought the noise was thunder so loud that it was deafening. I think she was right.

WACKY:

I would like to like the things you like, but it's not like me to like something just because somebody else likes it.

BETTER:

It would be nice if we liked the same things, but it's not my nature to pretend to enjoy something just because someone else does.

WACKY:

I spoke to my dad on the phone, and when I told him where I was, I was mad that he was mad that I was where I was.

BETTER:

I spoke to my dad on the phone. When I told him where I was, he was angry—and that made *me* angry!

WACKY:

Just as I rounded the corner, I saw an airplane circling very low around a tall, round building. I asked myself a round of questions including, what's going on around here?

BETTER:

Just as I turned the corner, I saw an airplane circling very low around a tall, circular building. I asked myself a series of questions including, what on earth is happening?

# Clichés

## Not that same old phrase again

*Blind as a bat, cool as a cucumber,* and *happy as a clam*—they are all clichés. A cliché is an overused expression. A million writers have used the expression before you, and a million will use it after you. So why use it?

With so many spicy words in the English language, usually you can come up with something more clever than the same-old same-old.

## Count the clichés in this story:

Last night I was hungry as a bear. I told my mom I wanted a really big dinner because I knew I could eat like a pig. She said, "Let's go to McDonald's."

We left the house in a flash, and Mom drove like a bat out of hell. As soon as we got to McDonald's, I could tell that something fishy was going on. There was not a soul to be seen. It was as plain as the nose on my face that they were closed for the duration, so we headed out for Bob's Grill.

Bob's Grill was neither closed nor crowded—in fact, there was room to spare. By that time I was hungry to beat the band, and I ordered enough barbecued ribs to choke a horse. When they came, I was up to my ears in ribs, but, believe it or not, I ate every last one.

Later in the evening I was sick as a dog. That just goes to show you: sometimes your eyes are bigger than your stomach. My mom gave me some Pepto Bismol, which I drank like water, and then I slept like a baby.

The moral of this story is this: go nice and easy when you order ribs at Bob's.

How many clichés did you count? Did you catch all of these?

| | |
|---|---|
| hungry as a bear | eat like a pig |
| in a flash | like a bat out of hell |
| something fishy going on | not a soul to be seen |
| as plain as the nose on my face | for the duration |
| headed out | room to spare |
| to beat the band | enough to choke a horse |
| up to my ears | believe it or not |
| every last one | sick as a dog |
| just goes to show you | your eyes are bigger than your stomach |
| drank like water | slept like a baby |
| the moral of the story | nice and easy |

## Caution—Major Mistake Territory!

Clichés aren't wrong; they're just worn out. Use them occasionally or for a special effect, but don't use many or your writing will be as soggy as a dishcloth (catch that one?). Be creative with your words.

Here are some more:

| | |
|---|---|
| crazy as a loon | rock the boat |
| easy as pie | muddy the water |
| high as a kite | have time to kill |
| skinny as a rail | down and out |
| smart as a whip | ripe old age |
| mad as a hornet | there's more in store |
| naked as a jay bird | raining cats and dogs |

| | |
|---|---|
| loose as a goose | down in the dumps |
| bright as a button | cry over spilled milk |
| hard as nails | heart-to-heart talk |
| strong as an ox | on the tip of your tongue |
| fresh as a daisy | take a rain check |
| thick as thieves | for crying out loud |
| tight as a drum | eat your heart out |

# Odds and ends

## Rambling paragraphs

It is not uncommon to see a book report or short paper written with only one paragraph. Don't do it! Rambling paragraphs are very difficult on your reader. Think about where one set of

ideas ends and another begins, and your paragraphs will fall
naturally into place.

## Cutesy writing

Whatever you do, for goodness gravy (tee-hee, just kidding),
pleez don't be 2 cute. It makes your writing look soooo . . .
ooooh, U know . . . silly.

## Spelling

Which is correct: *commitment, committment*, or *comittment*?
Which is correct: *occurrence, occurence*, or *occurance*? When it
comes to spelling, English can be a very strange language, so
check your spelling carefully. If a word looks phunny or wierd,
look it up.

Computer spelling checkers are the most wonderful things
since ice cream was invented. If you use one, however, you still
must proofread carefully. Computers don't know the difference
between *write, right*, and *rite*—they're all spelled correctly.

In a sentences that look lack thus, you're computer wood
nut sea any thin wrung because all these warts is spilled write.

# BRAIN TICKLERS
## *Set # 19*

Find the goofs in these sentences and correct
them.

1. I bought a great new coat for cold winter
   days. Tuesday was colder than the
   weatherman had said it would be, and I
   hadn't worn my coat. I was so cold I thought
   I'd die of cold!

2. Peter was at Debbie's house. He heard a
   strange sound. He went into the living room.

He was surprised to hear the parrot calling "out." Peter let the bird out. The parrot's name is Loud Mouth.

3. I needed a new jacket. Red is my favorite color. I bought a new jacket. It's red. I like it.

4. In ballet school, Katie and Kristen learn ballet technique, all about stage makeup, and how to choreograph dances.

5. I stayed up late studying for the math quiz, talking on the phone, and I had to pack for our trip.

6. Half the kids ordered hamburgers, half ordered chicken, and a few ordered tacos.

7. Today I need to work on my term paper, visit my grandmother, and cleaning up my room would earn me some points with Mom.

8. I'm dead tired, flat broke, and I'm having a bad hair day to boot.

(Answers are on page 258.)

# GETTING IT ALL TOGETHER: EDITING A PAPER

## Think, write, edit

### Now we're going to pull together everything we have learned in this book.

This is my first draft of a short piece about MTV for social studies class. It's a mess. Help me clean it up.

> Some people say that MTV is a real bad infleunce on kids. There are a number of other things people complain about: The amount of violence on the music videos, cussing in other shows, and some sexual themes in the music videos. Beavis and Butthead in particular have caused quite a reaction. They have been blamed for causing young kids to set fires one of which was fatile. But

245

MTV can't be considered all bad. It encourages kids to listen to music and gives them something to do besides hitting the streets. They also give advice about stuff like drugs and safe sex. If I was hired to change MTV, I'd make it less violent. I think that one thing would clean up most of its problems.

Step 1: Check spelling.

There are two spelling errors in this piece. Did you catch them? They are *infleunce* (that's *influence*) and *fatile* (that's *fatal*).

Step 2: Check for punctuation mistakes. There are four in this piece:

*They have been blamed for causing young kids to set fires one of which was fatal.* There should be a comma after *fires*.

*Beavis and Butthead in particular have caused quite a reaction.* There should be commas before and after *in particular*.

*Beavis and Butthead* should be in italics or underlined since it is the name of a television series.

After the colon in the second sentence, *the* is capitalized. However, the phrase following the colon is not a complete sentence, so *the* should be in lowercase. Also, a colon should not follow a preposition (*about* is a preposition). Let's reword the sentence to say, "There are a number of other things people complain about, including the following: . . . "

Step 3: Check for verb mistakes.

*Beavis and Butthead* is a television show (singular), not two individuals (plural). It should be *Beavis and Butthead, in particular, has caused quite a reaction* (not *have caused quite a reaction*). *It has been blamed* (not *they have been blamed*) . . .

*If I was hired* should be *if I were hired*. This is a case where the subjunctive should be used. Since I have not actually been hired to clean up MTV, this is a "what if" (in other words, subjunctive) type of statement.

Step 4: Check for adverb and adjective mistakes.

In the first sentence we have the phrase *real bad influence*. How bad? This question implies that an adverb is needed. *Real* is an adjective; *really* is an adverb.

Step 5: Check for unnecessary words.

In *some sexual themes in the music videos*, who needs the word *some*? Obviously there are some—if there were none, would I be mentioning them at all?

Step 6: Look for dumb statements.

There's one very dumb one here. All writers make dumb mistakes on the first draft—and sometimes on the second draft. The mistake is this: *There are a number of other things people complain about.* What *other* things? I haven't said anything yet, so how can there be *other* things?

Step 7: Look for colloquialisms, slang, informal phrases, and weak words.

*Stuff like drugs and safe sex*: Let's change that to *issues such as drugs and safe sex.*

*Hitting the streets*: Let's change that to *spending time being bored or being tempted by trouble.*

*Clean up:* Let's change that to *solve.*

*Cussing* should be *cursing.*

*MTV can't be considered all bad*: Let's change that to. *MTV can't be considered completely bad. Perhaps it has some redeeming qualities.*

Step 8:  Check paragraphing.

This is all one paragraph. Does it read well that way? No, so let's change that.

## After the first round of cleanup, this is what we have:

Some people say that MTV is a really bad influence on kids. There are a number of things people complain about, including the following: the amount of violence on the music videos, cursing in other shows, and sexual themes in the music videos. *Beavis and Butthead,* in particular, has caused quite a reaction. It has been blamed for causing young kids to set fires, one of which was fatal.

MTV can't be considered completely bad. Perhaps it has some redeeming qualities. It encourages kids to listen to music and gives them something to do besides spending time being bored or being tempted by trouble. They also give advice about issues such as drugs and safe sex.

If I were hired to change MTV, I'd make it less violent. I think that one thing would solve most of its problems.

It's better, but it's not good enough to suit me. Let's keep working on it.

Step 9:  Look for vague phrases.

*Some people say that MTV is a really bad influence on kids.* Which people? Politicians, teachers, advertisers, parents, or kids themselves? The focus is the writer's choice. In this piece, let's focus on parents.

*I think that one thing would solve most of its problems.* Why use words as vague as *thing* and *its,* especially in the punch line of the piece? Let's make it this: *I think that one change would solve most of the network's problems.*

Step 10:  Look for inconsistent phrases or sentences.

> *MTV can't be considered completely bad. Perhaps it has some redeeming qualities. It encourages kids to listen to music and gives them something to do besides spending time being bored or being tempted by trouble. They also give advice about issues such as drugs and safe sex.* Check out the underlining: MTV, it, it, they. Why the switch to *they?* Let's change *they* to *MTV*. Since *MTV* is a singular noun, the verb must be singular as well. So let's write *gives*.

Step 11: Look for repetition of words or phrases.

> *. . . the amount of violence on the music videos, cursing in other shows, and sexual themes in the music videos.* If we're talking about two aspects of music videos, why not join them? Let's make it *the amount of violence and the sexual themes on music videos and the cursing in other shows.*

> *If I were hired to change MTV, I'd make it less violent. I think that one change would solve most of the network's problems.* Two *changes* too close together. Not good. Which change do we want to change? I say let's go after the first one (although either is fine). What's another word? Let's check the thesaurus under *change*: overhaul, improve, rectify, correct. I like *overhaul*.

> *Beavis and Butthead, in particular, has caused quite a reaction. It has been blamed for causing young kids to set fires, one of which was fatal.* Did you catch this one? It's subtle, but good writers catch the subtle goofs: *caused* in one sentence and *causing* in the next sentence. Let's change one of them. *Beavis and Butthead, in particular, has caused quite a reaction. It has been blamed for inspiring young kids to set fires, one of which was fatal.*

## After the second round of cleanup, this is what we have:

> Some parents say that MTV is a really bad influence on kids. There are a number of things parents complain about, including the following: the amount of violence and the sexual themes on music videos and the cursing in other shows. *Beavis and Butthead*, in particular, has caused quite a reaction. It has been blamed for inspiring young kids to set fires, one of which was fatal.
>
> MTV can't be considered completely bad. Perhaps it has some redeeming qualities. It encourages kids to listen to music and gives them something to do besides spending time being bored or being tempted by trouble. MTV also gives advice about issues such as drugs and safe sex.
>
> If I were hired to overhaul MTV, I'd make it less violent. I think that one change would solve most of the network's problems.

This isn't bad. Would you stop here and turn it in? Not I—I'm just getting warmed up! Let's tear this piece apart word by word, looking for any weakling we can find.

> *Some parents say*—there's one. *Say* is weak; it can mean so many things: whimper, confess, scream, cry, whisper. What are the parents doing? They are certainly doing more than just *saying*. Are they shouting? Too intense for this piece. Are they suggesting? Too weak for this piece. How about *arguing*? I like it. (*Argue* here does not mean to fight with each other; it means "to strongly make a point.")

> *Some parents argue that MTV is a really bad influence.* There's another one. Can't we do better than *really bad*? What are the parents saying—that MTV is nasty? That it's disgusting, it's warping our kids' minds, its music is turning our children away from John Denver? Ask a

hundred people and you'd hear a hundred different opinions. What do these parents think is the bad influence? Let's try this: *Some parents argue that MTV is a potentially dangerous influence.* We are building up to discussing the violence on MTV, so let's hint at that in the beginning of the piece.

I spotted another weakling: *quite a reaction.* What kind of reaction? A street riot of thousands of parents? Hundreds of angry letters to the editor of the local newspaper? A whiny phone call from one kid's aunt? What are we talking about here? Let's try this: *a public outcry from around the country.*

Here's another one: *it has been blamed.* When? Why? How did it happen? Let's try this: *As a result of Beavis's and Butthead's behavior in several episodes of the show, it has been blamed for inspiring young kids to set fires, one of which was fatal.*

Here is another weakling: *MTV can't be considered completely bad.* According to whom? Let's be more specific: *I don't believe MTV is completely bad.*

*Perhaps it has some redeeming qualities.* Why say *perhaps*? Either it does or it doesn't have redeeming qualities—who wants to read a wishy-washy piece? Let's change it: *To its credit, MTV has some redeeming qualities. For example . . .*

*MTV also gives advice about issues such as drugs and safe sex.* Let's make this stronger: MTV also gives much-needed advice about issues such as drugs and safe sex—advice that kids may heed when they hear it from rock stars and other teen idols.

*I'd make it less violent.* This sentence has no muscle. How about this: *I would clean up Beavis's and Butthead's attitudes, lessen the cursing on the network, and slash the violence—reducing it by at least 50 percent.* Now there's a little muscle!

*If I were hired to overhaul MTV, I would clean up Beavis's and Butthead's attitudes, lessen the cursing, and slash the violence—reducing it by at least 50 percent. I think that one change would solve most of the network's problems.* We edited the next-to-last sentence to include three improvements, but the last sentence still refers to "that one change." More importantly, the conclusion fizzles; the final sentence is not as strong as the next-to-last sentence. This is the punch line of the piece, so we need to be clear, specific, and strong. How about this: *I believe that these few changes would help remove MTV from the field of potentially dangerous influences and make it a more healthy, creative, joyful entertainment for kids of all ages.* This sentence is much stronger, presents a clear opinion (it's not wishy-washy), ties the conclusion in with the introduction (the phrase about "potentially dangerous" links the two), and ends on a positive note rather than a depressing one.

## After the third round of cleanup, this is what we have:

Some parents argue that MTV is a potentially dangerous influence on kids. There are a number of things parents complain about, including the following: the amount of violence and the sexual themes on music videos and the cursing in other shows. *Beavis and Butthead,* in particular, has caused a public outcry from around the country. As a result of Beavis's and Butthead's behavior in several episodes of the show, it has been blamed for inspiring young kids to set fires, one of which was fatal.

I don't believe MTV is completely bad. To its credit, MTV has some redeeming qualities. For example, it encourages kids to listen to music and gives them something to do besides spending time being bored or being tempted by trouble. MTV also gives much-needed advice about issues such as drugs and safe sex—advice that kids may heed when they hear it from rock stars and other teen idols.

If I were hired to overhaul MTV, I would clean up Beavis's and Butthead's attitudes, lessen the cursing on the network, and slash the violence—reducing it by at least 50 percent. I believe that these few changes would help remove MTV from the field of potentially dangerous influences and make it a more healthy, creative, joyful entertainment for kids of all ages.

Finally, I'm happy with it. What do you think?

# BRAIN TICKLERS— THE ANSWERS

## Set # 17, page 222

1. Bring your rollerblades with you when you come to my house.

   There's nothing wrong with this sentence, but you can make it crisper by leaving out two words: Bring your rollerblades when you come to my house.

2. I rarely ever sleep late, but today I stayed in bed until noon.

   *Rarely ever* is a commonly used phrase, but it's double talk. I rarely sleep late, but today I stayed in bed until noon.

3. Dad's new car is a blue Ford with a black interior, with power steering and power brakes, and with an engine with six cylinders.

Who needs all those *with*'s? Dad's new car is a blue Ford with a black interior, power steering, power brakes, and a six-cylinder engine.

4. There are some people who pad their sentences with unnecessary words.

There's nothing wrong with this sentence, but this is much crisper: Some people pad their sentences with unnecessary words.

5. I got a flu shot yesterday. This is supposed to keep me from getting sick this winter.

Be suspicious of a *this is* sentence—many of them are weak and puny. I got a flu shot yesterday, which is supposed to keep me from getting sick this winter.

6. That movie is so cool; you'll just love it.

Fine for conversation, puny for a language arts paper. That movie is outstanding; you'll love it.

7. I am sort of tired.

*Sort of* is puny. I am a little tired.

8. I like Bill better than Frank.

Some words are missing. Which of these do you mean?
- I like Bill better than Frank likes Bill.
- I like Bill better than I like Frank.

9. I know you want to go ice skating. I also want to go ice skating, too.

The second sentence contains double talk. *Also* and *too* mean exactly the same thing. Both of these are correct:

- I want to go ice skating, too.
- I also want to go ice skating.

10. It has seldom been the case that I have vacuumed my room without Mom's prodding me.

    Too wordy. Seldom have I vacuumed my room without Mom's prodding me.

11. There are many reasons why you should eat plenty of vegetables.

    The problem here is double talk. Knock out *why* and the sentence will be fine. There are many reasons you should eat plenty of vegetables.

12. I need to get me something to eat.

    What's that *me* doing there? Both of these are correct:
    - I need to get something to eat.
    - I need to get myself something to eat.

13. I have never and probably will never be a brave bungee jumper.

    A necessary word has been left out. I have never been and probably will never be a brave bungee jumper.

14. Pat is smarter than all the boys in the class.

    A word might be missing. If Pat is a girl, this sentence is perfect. If Pat is a boy, it should be this: Pat is smarter than all the other boys in the class.

15. The reason I did poorly on the test is because my dog ate my study sheets.

    *The reason is because* is double talk. Both of these are correct:
    - The reason I did poorly on the test is that my dog ate my study sheets.
    - I did poorly on the test because my dog ate my study sheets.

## Set # 18, page 233

1. The doctor said that if I don't start eating something other than Hershey bars within a month my brain will be solid chocolate.

   The phrase *within a month* is confusing. Do you need to start eating better within a month, or will your brain be chocolate within a month? Both of these are correct:
   - The doctor said that if I don't start eating something other than Hershey bars within a month, my brain will be solid chocolate. (Notice that the comma makes it clear.)
   - The doctor said that if I don't start eating something other than Hershey bars, my brain will be solid chocolate within a month.

2. That movie is unlike none other I've seen.

   *Unlike none* is a double negative. These are both correct:
   - That movie is like none other I've seen.
   - That movie is unlike any other I've seen.

3. I have never thought of myself as a nobody accomplishing nothing in life.

   This sentence is actually correct even though it contains three negatives: *never*, *nobody*, and *nothing*. All those negatives make the sentence difficult to read. This is better: I never think of myself as someone who accomplishes little in life.

4. I went to visit my cousin in Atlanta because my parents were going on a trip to California, a trip they had looked forward to for a long time, and my cousin and I, along with several of her friends, had a great time shopping, seeing movies, and doing other things, like water skiing and snorkeling, that I had wanted to do for a long time but hadn't had a chance to do because my parents said it was more important for me to focus on school work, especially on improving my writing skills.

   Whew! If that run-on sentence ran on any longer, it could fill an entire book. Try breaking it into three or four separate sentences.

5. Ryan led his pet alligator, holding his head high with pride, into the winner's circle at the pet show.

   Who is holding his head high—Ryan or the alligator? Ryan, holding his head high with pride, led his pet alligator into the winner's circle at the pet show.

6. Teresa watched the lion approach wide-eyed with fear.

   It sounds as though the lion is scared of Teresa! Wide-eyed with fear, Teresa watched the lion approach.

7. Johnny is so sleepy he doesn't hardly remember his own name.

   The problem is a double negative: does *not hardly*. Johnny is so sleepy he hardly remembers his own name.

8. I told my mom I wanted to go to the mall to buy some supplies for my science project, and that is what happened.

   *And that is what happened* is very vague. What happened? You told your mom or you went to the mall? I told my mom I wanted to go to the mall to buy some supplies for my science project, so she took me.

9. I said a few nasty things to my parents that I'm not proud of.

   It sounds as though you're not proud of your parents. I think you mean this: I said a few nasty things that I'm not proud of to my parents.

10. Mom served dessert to my friends on paper plates.

    Your friends were on paper plates? I'd like to see that! Mom served dessert on paper plates to my friends.

11. I like your dress.

    Nothing is wrong here, but could this sentence use some vitamins? Maybe this: The colors and style of your new dress are gorgeous.

12. I think that maybe we should do something to improve the conditions of some people who are in some sort of trouble.

   Thick fog! We who? Do what? For what people? What conditions and what sort of trouble? Be specific and be clear. This is one possibility: I firmly believe that our government should do more to improve the living conditions of migrant farm workers.

13. Man, we're really cooking now!

   This is some major slang. You have to decide if it's appropriate or not. If it's not, try this: We're really making progress now!

## Set # 19, page 244

1. I bought a great new coat for cold winter days. Tuesday was colder than the weatherman had said it would be, and I hadn't worn my coat. I was so cold I thought I'd die of cold!

   The word *cold* is used four times. Try this: I bought a great new coat for winter days. Tuesday was colder than the weatherman had said it would be, and I hadn't worn my coat. I thought I'd freeze!

2. Peter was at Debbie's house. He heard a strange sound. He went into the living room. He was surprised to hear the parrot calling "out." Peter let the bird out. The parrot's name is Loud Mouth.

   This paragraph is very choppy. There are many possible ways to improve it. Here is one way: While he was at Debbie's house, Peter heard a strange sound coming from the living room. When he realized that the sound was Loud Mouth, Debbie's parrot, calling "out," Peter let the bird out of the cage.

3. I needed a new jacket. Red is my favorite color. I bought a new jacket. It's red. I like it.

This is so choppy it sounds like something a five-year-old would write. Try something juicier. Red is my favorite color, so when I needed a new jacket, I chose a beautiful one in a soft shade of rose.

4. In ballet school, Katie and Kristen learn ballet technique, all about stage makeup, and how to choreograph dances.

   This is not consistent. In ballet school, Katie and Kristen learn ballet technique [noun], methods [noun] of applying stage makeup, and choreography [noun].

5. I stayed up late studying for the math quiz, talking on the phone, and I had to pack for our trip.

   This is not consistent. I stayed up late studying for the math quiz, talking on the phone, and packing for our trip.

6. Half the kids ordered hamburgers, half ordered chicken, and a few ordered tacos.

   Wake up, brain cells, wake up! How many kids does this make?

7. Today I need to work on my term paper, visit my grand-mother, and cleaning up my room would earn me some points with Mom.

   This is not consistent. Here is one way to fix it: Today I need . . . Today I need to work on my term paper, visit my grandmother, and clean up my room if I want to earn some points with Mom.

8. I'm dead tired, flat broke, and I'm having a bad hair day to boot.

   One sentence, four clichés: *dead tired, flat broke, bad hair day,* and *to boot.* Since this is the last exercise of the book, let's let sleeping dogs lie (another cliché) and call it quits (another cliché). Whatta ya have to say about that (another cliché)?

# INDEX